Englisch für das Hotel- und Gaststättengewerbe

Material
Elementary
Intermediate
Advanced

von
Jürgen Haase
Günter Neis

winklers verlag

42681

Vorwort

Das vorliegende Lehrwerk *Englisch für das Hotel- und Gaststättengewerbe* stellt eine Übungssammlung dar, mit deren Hilfe den Auszubildenden dieser Branche die für die erfolgreiche Ausübung ihrer Tätigkeit notwendigen englischen Sprachmittel an die Hand gegeben werden. Im Mittelpunkt steht also die Bewältigung von regelmäßig vorkommenden Kommunikationssituationen mit Englisch sprechenden Gästen und nicht die systematische Einübung sprachlicher Strukturen. Die behandelten Situationen entstammen der beruflichen Wirklichkeit des Hotel- und Restaurantpersonals im deutschsprachigen Raum (nicht dazu gehört z. B. ein Londoner Stadtplan, ebenso wenig die englischsprachige Speisenkarte eines amerikanischen Restaurants – die lediglich unter landeskundlichen Aspekten von Interesse wären).

Da wir davon ausgehen, dass die Schülerinnen und Schüler mehr oder weniger ausführliche Englischkenntnisse mitbringen, handelt es sich bei *Englisch für das Hotel- und Gaststättengewerbe* nicht um einen Kurs zum Erlernen der englischen Sprache. Es finden sich deswegen auch **keine Grammatikübungen**, da für uns nicht abzusehen ist, welche grammatikalischen Phänomene im individuellen Fall zu wiederholen und zu üben sind.

Auf eine inhaltliche Progression haben wir verzichtet, da sich das Vorgehen der Lehrerin/des Lehrers nach den jeweiligen Gegebenheiten vor Ort – Stoffverteilungspläne, Unterrichtsorganisation (Teilzeit-, Block- oder Projektunterricht) usw. – richten muss. **Alle Kapitel stehen gleichberechtigt nebeneinander**, d. h., die Lehrerin/der Lehrer kann entscheiden, wann welches Thema im Laufe des Unterrichts behandelt wird.

Da die Vorkenntnisse in Englisch von Fall zu Fall aller Erfahrung nach sehr unterschiedlich sein können, haben wir dieses Lehrwerk auf drei unterschiedlichen Niveaus organisiert.

Die zum Einsatz kommenden **Materialien** sind für die Schülerinnen und Schüler aller Niveaus gleich – ausgehend von der Überlegung, dass die Situationen, mit denen die Auszubildenden konfrontiert werden, ja auch für alle gleich sind. Die auf den Materialien basierenden Übungen sind dann im Schwierigkeitsgrad einem der drei Niveaus **Elementary, Intermediate** und **Advanced** angepasst. Auch das zum Einsatz kommende Vokabular ist im Umfang auf das jeweilige Niveau abgestimmt. In den **Vokabellisten** am Ende findet sich jedoch das relevante Gesamtvokabular als Nachschlagemöglichkeit für alle Schüler.

Für Schulen, die den Englischunterricht in Kursen, Lerngruppen o. Ä. organisieren können, deren Zusammensetzung an der Vorbildung der Schülerinnen und Schüler orientiert ist, bietet sich hier die Möglichkeit, die Auszubildenden ihrem jeweiligen Niveau entsprechend zu unterrichten. Die Präsentation der **drei Niveaus in einem Band** ermöglicht es, darüber hinaus auf leistungsstärkere bzw. -schwächere Schülerinnen und Schüler einzugehen, indem ihnen aus einem anderen Niveau Übungen zur Bearbeitung gegeben werden.

Sollte eine Differenzierung des Unterrichts in verschiedene Lerngruppen nicht möglich sein, kann dieses Lehrwerk bei Bedarf auch binnendifferenzierend eingesetzt werden, da ja alle Schülerinnen und Schüler mit den gleichen Materialien die gleichen Aufgaben zu bewältigen hätten, wenn auch jeweils auf einem ihrer Vorbildung angemessenen Niveau. Auch in diesem Fall ist ein individuelles Eingehen auf die Schüler mit Übungen eines anderen Niveaus natürlich möglich.

Da das internationale Englisch zweifelsohne vom amerikanischen Englisch bestimmt wird, wurde das Vokabular in erster Linie am *American English* ausgerichtet. Im Text werden unter anderem folgende Abkürzungen verwendet: AE (amerikanisches Englisch), BE (britisches Englisch), MZ (Mehrzahl).

Frühjahr 2004 *Die Autoren*

2. Auflage, 2004
© Winklers Verlag im Westermann Schulbuchverlag GmbH
Postfach 11 15 52, 64230 Darmstadt
Telefon: 06151 8768-0 Fax: 06151 8768-61
http://www.winklers.de
Druck: westermann druck GmbH, Braunschweig
ISBN 3-8045-4268-9

Inhaltsverzeichnis

Materialien

Übungen

Vokabular

M1

Vorbereitungsarten – ways of preparation			
anmachen (Salat)	*to toss*	angemacht mit ...	*tossed in ...*
aromatisieren	*to flavor, (BE) flavour*	aromatisiert	*flavored, (BE) flavoured*
aromatisieren (mit Spirituosen)	*to lace*	aromatisiert (mit Spirituosen)	*laced*
beträufeln	*to sprinkle*	beträufelt	*sprinkled*
dekorieren	*to decorate*	dekoriert	*decorated*
einhüllen	*to wrap* [ræp], *to encase*	eingehüllt	*wrapped* [ræpt], *encased*
füllen	*to fill*	gefüllt	*filled*
füllen, stopfen	*to stuff*	gefüllt, gestopft	*stuffed*
garnieren	*to garnish*	garniert	*garnished*
glasieren	*to glaze*	glasiert	*glazed*
gratinieren	*to gratinate*	gratiniert	*gratinated, au gratin*
krönen	*to crown*	gekrönt	*crowned*
marinieren	*to marinade, to marinate*	mariniert	*marinaded, marinated*
mischen	*to mix*	gemischt	*mixed*
schlagen	*to whip, to beat*	geschlagen	*whipped, beaten*
servieren	*to serve*	serviert	*served*
tränken	*to soak*	getränkt	*soaked*
umhüllen, ummanteln	*to coat, to encase*	umhüllt, ummantelt	*coated, encased*
würzen	*to season*	gewürzt	*seasoned*

M2

Schneidearten – ways of cutting			
durch den Wolf drehen	*to grind, (BE) to mince*	durch den Wolf gedreht	*ground, (BE) minced*
filetieren/filieren	*to fillet* [fɪlɪt]	filetiert/filiert	*filleted* [ˈfɪlɪtɪd]
hacken	*to chop*	gehackt	*chopped*
in Scheiben schneiden	*to slice*	in Scheiben geschnitten	*sliced*
schneiden (in ...)	*to cut (into ...)*	geschnitten (in ...)	*cut (into ...)*
würfeln	*to cube/to dice*	gewürfelt	*cubed/diced*

M3

Garverfahren – ways of cooking			
garen	*to cook*	gegart	*cooked*
backen	*to bake*	gebacken	*baked*
braten (kurz)	*to fry*	gebraten (kurz)	*fried*
braten (lang)	*to roast*	gebraten (lang)	*roast*
dämpfen	*to steam*	gedämpft	*steamed*
dünsten	*to stew*	gedünstet	*stewed*
frittieren	*to deep-fry*	frittiert	*deep-fried*
grillen	*to broil, (BE) to grill*	gegrillt	*broiled, (BE) grilled*
kochen *(bei 100 °C in Wasser garen)*	*to boil*	gekocht *(bei 100 °C in Wasser gegart)*	*boiled*
pochieren *(bei 80 – 90 °C in Wasser garen)*	*to poach*	pochiert *(bei 80 – 90 °C in Wasser gegart)*	*poached*
schmoren	*to braise*	gebraten, geschmort – Rinder(schmor)braten – Schweine(...)braten – ...braten	*braised* *- braised beef* *- braised pork* *- braised ...*

M4

Fleischteile – pieces of meat

Brust	*breast*	Schinken	*ham*
Filet	*fillet* ['fɪlɪt]	Schnitzel	*escalope* ['eskəlɒp]
Hachse/Haxe	*knuckle* ['nʌkl]	Speck	*bacon*
Keule	*leg*	Steak – Hüftsteak – Rumpsteak	*steak* *- rumpsteak* *- sirloin steak*
Kotelett	*cutlet*		
Rücken	*saddle*		

M5

Fleisch – meat

Pferd(efleisch)	*horsemeat*	Schaf(fleisch) – Hammel(fleisch) – Lamm(fleisch)	*mutton* *- mutton* *- lamb* [læm]
Rind(fleisch) – Kalb(fleisch) – Ochsenfleisch	*beef* *- veal* *- beef*	Schwein(efleisch)	*pork*

M6

Tiere – animals

Rind – Kalb – Ochse	cow *- calf* [kæf, (BE) kɒːf] *- ox*	Schaf – Lamm	sheep *- lamb* [læm]
		Schwein – Spanferkel	pig *- suckling pig*

M7

Innereien – offal			
Bries	*sweetbread*	Lunge	*(MZ) lights*
Herz	*heart*	Mark	*marrow*
Hirn	*brain*	Niere	*kidney*
Leber	*liver*	Zunge	*tongue* [tʌŋ]

M8

Geflügel – poultry ['pəʊltrɪ]			
Ente	*duck*	Puter, Truthahn	*turkey*
Gans/Gänse	*goose* [guːs]/*geese* [giːs]	Strauß	*ostrich* ['ɒstrɪtʃ]
Huhn	*chicken*		

M9

Wildbret – game / Federwild – feathered game			
Elch - amerikanischer Elch - europäischer Elch	 - *moose* [muːs] - *elk*	Rebhuhn Taube	*partridge* *pigeon* ['pɪdʒɪn]
Fasan	*pheasant* ['feznt]	Wachtel	*quail*
Hase	*hare*	Wild (Fleisch)	*venison* ['venɪzn]
Kaninchen	*rabbit*	Wildschwein	*wild boar*
Perlhuhn	*guinea fowl* ['gɪnɪfaʊl]		

Fisch – fish three fish (Anzahl) / three fishes (Arten)

M10

Süßwasserfische – freshwater fishes	
Aal	*eel*
Forelle	*trout*
Hecht	*pike*
Karpfen	*carp*
Lachs	*salmon* ['sæmən]
Schleie	*tench*
Stör	*sturgeon*
Zander	*perch-pike, pike-perch*

M11

Salzwasserfische – sea fishes	
Heilbutt	*halibut*
Hering	*herring*
Kabeljau	*cod*
Makrele	*mackerel*
Sardelle	*anchovy/-ies*
Sardine	*sardine*
Schellfisch	*haddock*
Scholle	*plaice* [pleɪs]
Seeteufel (Lotte)	*angler fish*
Seezunge	*sole*
Steinbutt	*turbot*
Thunfisch	*tuna*
Tintenfisch	*calamari*

M12

Krusten- und Schaltiere – shellfish			
Austern	*oysters*	Languste	*crawfish*
Garnelen	*shrimps*	Miesmuscheln	*mussels*
Hummer	*lobster*	Steingarnelen	*prawns*
Jakobsmuscheln	*scallops*	Strandkrabbe	*crab*
Krebs	*crayfish*	Venusmuscheln	*clams*

M13

Gemüse – vegetables

Artischocke	*artichoke*
Aubergine	*aubergine, (BE) egg plant*
Bohnen	*beans*
- Dicke Bohnen	*- broad beans*
- Grüne Bohnen	*- French beans*
- Sojabohnen	*- soybeans*
Chicorée	*Belgian endive* ['endaɪv], *(BE) chicory* ['tʃɪkərɪ]
Endivie	*endive* ['endaɪv]
Erbsen	*peas*
- Kaiserschoten/ Zuckererbsen	*- sugar peas*
Feldsalat	*lamb's lettuce*
Fenchel	*fennel*
Gewürzgurke	*pickle, (BE) gherkin*
Gurke	*cucumber* ['kjuːkʌmbə]
Kartoffel(n)	*potato(es)*
- Bratkartoffeln	*- fried potatoes*
- Folienkartoffel	*- baked jacket potato*
- Kartoffelbrei	*- mashed potatoes*
- Kartoffelkroketten	*- potato croquettes/ croquette potatoes*
- Pommes frites	*- French fries, (BE) chips*
- Pellkartoffeln	*- boiled jacket potatoes*
- Salzkartoffeln	*- boiled potatoes*
Knoblauch	*garlic*
Kohl	*cabbage*
- Blumenkohl	*- cauliflower* ['kɒlɪflaʊər]
- Brokkoli	*- broccoli*
- Chinakohl	*- Chinese cabbage*
- Grünkohl	*- curly/green kale*
- Kohlrabi	*- kohlrabi*
- Rosenkohl	*- Brussel(s) sprouts*
- Rotkohl	*- red cabbage*
- Sauerkraut	*- sauerkraut* ['saʊəkraʊt]
- Weißkohl	*- white cabbage*
- Wirsing	*- Savoy cabbage*
Kürbis	*pumpkin*
Lauch, Porree	*leek*
Mais	*corn, (BE) maize*
Mangold	*(Swiss) chard*
Meerrettich	*horseradish*
Möhre	*carrot*
Olive	*olive*
Paprika	*(sweet) peppers*
Pastinake	*parsnip*
Pilz	*mushroom*
- Champignon	*- champignon, mushroom*
- Wiesenchampignon	*- field mushroom*
- Zuchtchampignon	*- button mushroom*
- Morchel	*- morel*
- Pfifferling	*- chanterelle*
- Steinpilz	*- (flat) mushroom*
- Trüffel	*- truffle*

M13

Gemüse – vegetables			
Porree/Lauch	*leek*	Schwarzwurzeln	*black salsify* ['sælsɪfɪ]
Radieschen	*radish/-es*	Spargel – Spargelspitzen	*asparagus* [ə'spærəgəs] – *asparagus tips*
Rhabarber	*rhubarb* ['ruːbɑːb]	Spinat	*spinach* ['spɪnɪtʃ, (BE) 'spɪnɪdʒ]
Rote Bete	*beetroot*	Tomate(n)	*tomato(es)*
Rübe/weiße Rübe	*turnip*	Zucchini	*zucchini, (BE) courgette*
Salat	*lettuce* ['letɪs]	Zwiebel	*onion* ['ʌnɪən]
Seetang	*seaweed*		
Sellerie (Stangen~)	*celery*		
Sellerie (Knollen~)	*celariac* [sə'lɪərɪæk], *German celery*		

M14

Getreide – corn			
Dinkel	*spelt*	Mais	*corn, (BE) maize*
Gerste	*barley*	Reis	*rice*
Hafer	*oats*	Roggen	*rye*
Hirse – indische Hirse – Mohrenhirse	*millet* – *dhurra, durra* – *sorghum*	Weizen	*wheat*

M15

Obst – fruit	
Ananas	*pineapple*
Apfel	*apple*
Apfelsine	*orange*
Aprikose	*apricot* ['eɪprɪkɒt]
Backplaume	*prune*
Banane	*banana*
Beere(n)	*berry/-ies*
Birne	*pear* [peər]
Blaubeere(n), Heidelbeere(n) – amer. Heidelbeere(n)	*blueberry/-ies* – *huckleberry/-ies*
Brombeere(n)	*blackberry/-ies*
Dattel	*date*
Erdbeere(n)	*strawberry/-ies*
Erdnuss	*peanut*
Esskastanie, Marone	*chestnut*
Feige	*fig*
Grapefruit	*grapefruit*
Haselnuss	*hazelnut*
Heidelbeere(n)/ Blaubeere(n) – amer. Heidelbeere(n)	*blueberry/-ies* – *huckleberry/-ies*
Himbeere(n)	*raspberry/-ies*
Honigmelone	*honeydew melon*
Johannisbeere (rote)	*red currant*
Johannisbeere (schwarze)	*black currant*
Kirsche(n)	*cherry/-ies*
Kokosnuss	*coconut*
Limette	*lime*
Mandel	*almond* ['ɑːmənd]
Marone, Esskastanie	*chestnut*
Melone	*melon*
Pampelmuse	*grapefruit*
Pfirsich(e)	*peach/-es*
Pflaume	*plum*
Pistazie	*pistachio* [pi'stɑː(æ)ʃiəʊ]
Preiselbeere(n)	*cranberry/-ies*
Quitte	*quince*
Rosine	*raisins*
Traube	*grapes*
Walnuss	*walnut*
Wassermelone	*water melon*
Weintraube	*grapes*
Zitrone	*lemon*

426812

M16

Kräuter – herbs / Gewürze – spices			
Anis	*aniseed*	Piment	*pimento*
Basilikum	*basil* ['bæzəl]	Pistazie	*pistachio* [pi'stɑː(æ)ʃiəʊ]
Beifuß	*mugwort*	Portulak	*purslane*
Bohnenkraut	*(summer) savory*	Rosmarin	*rosemary*
Borretsch	*borage*	Safran	*saffron*
Brennnessel	*stinging nettle*	Salbei	*sage*
Cayennepfeffer	*Cayenne/~ pepper*	Sauerampfer	*sorrel*
Chili	*chile, (BE) chilli*	Schalotte	*shallot*
Dill	*dill*	Schnittlauch	*chives*
Estragon	*tarragon*	Thymian	*thyme* ['taim]
Fenchel	*fennel*	Vanille	*vanilla*
Ingwer	*ginger* ['dʒɪndʒər]	Wacholderbeere(n)	*juniper berry/-ies*
Kerbel	*chervil*	Waldmeister	*woodruff*
Knoblauch	*garlic*	Zimt	*cinnamon*
Kümmel	*caraway seed*		
Löwenzahn	*dandelion* ['dændɪlaɪən]		
Lorbeerblatt (-blätter)	*bay leaf/leaves*		
Majoran	*marjoram*		
Minze	*mint*		
Mohn	*poppy seed*		
Muskatnuss	*nutmeg*		
Nelke	*clove*		
Nelkenpfeffer	*pimento*		
Oregano	*oregano*		
Paprika (Pulver)	*paprika*		
Petersilie	*parsley*		
Pfeffer	*pepper*		

M17

Zum Roten Ochsen

Tageskarte
20. März

Suppen

1. Tomatencremesuppe	4,00 €
2. Gemüsesuppe	4,00 €
3. Klare Brühe	4,00 €

Hauptgerichte

4. Schweinsbratwurst mit Kartoffelsalat[1]	6,30 €
5. Eisbein mit Kartoffelbrei und Sauerkraut	7,40 €
6. Wiener Schnitzel mit gemischtem Gemüse und Pommes frites	8,60 €
7. Rindersteak vom Grill mit Folienkartoffel und Bohnen	15,00 €
8. Leber Berliner Art mit Kartoffelbrei	7,00 €
9. Kalbszunge mit Spargel und Salzkartoffeln	8,20 €

Gerichte 6, 7, 9 mit gemischtem Salat

Nachtisch

10. Vanilleeis mit heißen Kirschen[2]	3,10 €
11. Rote Grütze mit Vanillesoße[2]	3,10 €
12. Obstsalat[1/2/3]	2,80 €

1 mit Konservierungsmitteln
2 mit Farbstoff
3 mit Süßstoff

M18

Vorspeisen

Gefüllte Tomaten

Wir servieren Ihnen zarteste Freilandtomaten mit einer fein abgestimmten Füllung aus köstlichen Bananen, fruchtiger Ananas und einer Mischung erlesener Nüsse. Abgerundet wird diese Komposition von einer mit ein wenig Zitrone aromatisierten erfrischenden Creme.

€ 10,00

Salade Gourmande

Auf einem Nest gefrosteter Salatblätter erwartet Sie ein Arrangement aus Wachteleiern, Entenleber und Waldpilzen, fein abgestimmt mit einem außergewöhnlichen Walnuss-Dressing.

€ 13,00

Carpaccio

Unsere milde Vinaigrette sowie am Tisch frisch gehobelter Parmesan machen die hauchdünnen Scheiben zartesten rohen Filets von französischen Charolais-Rindern zu einem exquisiten Genuss.

€ 14,50

Lauchcremesuppe

Pikant-milder Lauch und Kartoffeln aus neuer Ernte sind mit Schlagsahne zu einem herzhaft-delikaten Genuss vereint.

€ 7,50

M19

Fisch & Meeresfrüchte

Saumon au Poireau

Ein gedämpftes Steak von in Schottland gezüchtetem Lachs
wird gekrönt von einer Krabben-Mousse
und begleitet von einer leichten Lauchsoße.
Als ergänzende Beilage bieten wir Ihnen dazu
eine Auswahl an jungen Gemüsen.

€ 18,50 / € 21,50

Heilbutt holländische Art

Ein Steak vom Heilbutt
pochiert unser Küchenchef
in einer traditionellen Court-bouillon.
Dazu reichen wir Ihnen
eine fein abgestimmte holländische Soße.

€ 14,00 / € 18,50

Meeresfrüchte im Körbchen

Eine Auswahl frischer Meeresfrüchte,
pochiert in einer delikaten Safran-Tomaten-Essenz,
servieren wir Ihnen in einem Körbchen aus locker-leichtem
hausgemachtem Blätterteig.

€ 13,50 / € 16,00

Der letztgenannte Preis bezieht sich jeweils auf ein
Fischgericht als Hauptgang.

M20

Fleisch

Kräuterhühnchen

Zart gebratene Hühnchenbrust füllen wir für Sie
mit einer feinen Mousse aus selbst gezogener Brunnenkresse.
Umgeben wird dieser Genuss von einer ungewöhnlichen
Soße aus Gemüse, Weißwein sowie frischen Kräutern.
Die begleitende Beilage wählen Sie selbst aus unserem Angebot an
marktfrischem Gemüse.

€ 17,50

Entrecôte

Dieses saftig zarte Zwischenrippenstück mit dem typischen
Fettauge braten wir nach Ihren Wünschen
„englisch", „medium" oder „gut durch".
Dazu servieren wir goldbraun fritierte Kartoffelkroketten
und zarteste Prinzessböhnchen im Speckmantel.
Ergänzt wird dieses kräftige Gericht durch eine Mischung
knackigster Blattsalate mit einem Dressing Ihrer Wahl:
Estragon-Dressing, Roquefort-Dressing oder Joghurt-Dressing.

€ 25,50

Rehmedaillons

Unsere rosa gebratenen Rehmedaillons
finden auf ideale Weise ein köstliches Complément in
einer herbfruchtigen Wacholderbeersoße.
Kräftige Schwarzbrotknödel präsentieren sich als
schmackhafte Begleiter.

€ 27,80

M21

Vegetarische Genüsse

Blumenkohl im Teigmantel

Wir servieren Ihnen Röschen vom jungen Blumenkohl und fein gehackte Walnüsse, ummantelt mit einer goldbraun gebackenen Teigkruste, und präsentieren Ihnen diese fleischlose Komposition auf einer leichten Cremesoße.

€ 20,00

M21

Desserts

Mini-Erdbeer-Savarins

Ein lockeres, mit Rum getränktes Savarin bildet eine elegante Ergänzung zu köstlich süßen Erdbeeren und einer Dekoration aus frisch geschlagener Sahne.

€ 10,50

Citrus-Mandel-Traum

Unsere delikat-leichte Creme mit Zitrone und Mandeln vermählt sich harmonisch mit einer zartbitteren Mokkasoße.

€ 9,00

Tiramisú

Selbst in ihrem Heimatland werden Sie an unsere mit Likör aromatisierte Création aus italienischem Frischkäse, Löffelbiskuit, Kaffee und geschlagenem Eiweiß voller Sehnsucht zurückdenken.

€ 14,50

M23

Tageskarte

Gebeizter oder geräucherter norwegischer Lachs
€ 8,20

Honigmelone mit Schwarzwälder Rauchschinken
€ 6,00

Entenkraftbrühe mit Roter Bete

€ 5,30

Ragout von Schnecken und Pilzen

€ 6,50

Seezungenfilets in Weißweinsoße
mit kanadischem Wildreis

€ 11,00

Kalbsrückensteak
mit Senfkörnern, Blattspinat und Pommes frites

€ 14,30

Geschnetzeltes Schweinefilet
in Gorgonzolarahm mit Gemüsebukett und Kartoffelkroketten

€ 15,30

Entenbrust mit Mandelsoße
und Kartoffel-Birnen-Gratin

€ 15,30

Entrecôte
mit Burgunderzwiebeln, frischem Rosenkohl und Röstkartoffeln

€ 16,40

Geschmorte Lammkeule
mit Kräutern der Provence, Ratatouille und Kartoffelgratin

€ 16,50

Flambierte Schattenmorellen auf Vanillecreme
€ 7,20

Warmer französischer Apfelkuchen mit Karamellsoße
€ 7,20

M24

When guests from other countries are in Germany they very often want to try German food. But sometimes it can be that international guests of 'your' restaurant or hotel are not interested in it. The farther away from Central Europe a guest's home country the more different is her or his culture and the more different is the food she or he is used to.

So you might find it helpful to have some basic ideas about several national cuisines and so about the things a guest may be used to and may prefer. If you know a bit about those things you can more easily recommend a dish or a drink. Your guest will probably be very thankful.

You will notice that we do not say anything about French and Italian food. We think that in Central Europe these two national cuisines are so well known that telling you about them is really not necessary.

Great Britain & Ireland

The most famous items of the cuisine in the United Kingdom are obviously 'English Breakfast' and 'Five O'Clock Tea'.

An English breakfast is not only – as you know it from the "Continental Breakfast" served in hotels – rolls, jam and maybe some cold cuts or cheese. It begins with some cereals: traditionally porridge (i.e. oatmeal boiled in milk or water), but people prefer something like cornflakes, rice crispies etc. This cereal is followed by a mixed grill with fried or scrambled eggs, bacon, beef or pork sausages, grilled tomatoes, baked beans, mushrooms etc. – whatever people like. Toast with marmalade or jam is the end of the breakfast. Tea or coffee are the drinks that go with this meal. Of course you can add anything you like: fruit, fruit or vegetable juices; steak or fried potatoes for the mixed grill; honey, chocolate spread and ... and ... and ...

Tea – which does not have to be served exactly at five o'clock – is not to be confused with what we call in German *Kaffeeklatsch*; 'tea' is a substantial meal in itself. As the Britons used to have a very good and solid breakfast, lunch never was regarded as an important meal. As a consequence they were hungry again in the afternoon so that about that time it was high time for some calories. What you get nowadays when you order 'tea' in a hotel is kind of a 'three course meal': sandwiches (with cucumbers, watercress, anchovy-paste ...), scones (with butter or – more typical – with clotted cream and fruit preserve, i.e. jam), cake(s) and of course a pot of tea or coffee. 'High Tea' in the north of **England** and **Scotland** has even more courses: in addition to the above they eat fish, meat, puddings, desserts etc.

The **Britons** do not eat so much pork but beef and mutton or lamb. As a rule, vegetables are only boiled and served without a sauce.

The preferred meat in **Ireland** is sheep's meat and potatoes come with everything.

A very popular item in **Great Britain** as well as in **Ireland** are puddings: dishes cooked in a mould. There is almost no limit to the variety of puddings you can find on these islands: steak and kidney pudding, black pudding (what we call *Blutwurst*), Yorkshire pudding, rice pudding, plum pudding (strangely enough you will search in vain for plums in it). Almost the same recipes are used for making pies, which are more or less puddings covered by pastry.

Fish – cooked in a lot of different ways – is very popular as well among both peoples.

426820

Scandinavia

The most prominent items of the Scandinavian cuisine are, of course, fish and shellfish which are done in many ways: hot or cold, cooked or just marinaded or smoked – but never raw as in the Japanese tradition. However, the type of fish that is peferred differs from country to country: in **Norway** it is salmon and cod, in **Sweden** it is herring. The **Danes** surprisingly do not eat so much fish – they export most of what they catch; this is why in **Denmark** people eat very much pork.

Danish, **Norwegian** or **Swedish** guests would be delighted if you offered them venison – if you have it – as it plays an important role in their cuisine as well.

If Scandinavian guests do not like to try German food it may very well be that they love open sandwiches (called *smørrebrød* in **Danish** and *smorbrod* in Norwegian): in Scandinavia they are mostly on the basis of rye bread to which almost anything can be added – first of all, naturally, fish.

Eastern Europe

What plays a very important role in a **Russian** meal with several courses is a number of *sakuski*, i.e. appetizers, which are mainly fish, meat, eggs, marinaded or pickled vegetables and of course bread. There are absolutely no limits if you try to prepare and combine them; almost everything goes together.

In **Russia** soups, almost always purely vegetarian meals (or with fish), are often very rich on the one hand, on the other hand they can be very fine as a second course after the *sakuski*.

Since Eastern Europe is in large parts covered by woods, it is not surprising to find all sorts of mushrooms in the cuisines of those countries: in the early fall of course they are eaten fresh, right out of the vast forests. **Russia** is the only country that has developed a tradition of preserving mushrooms by marinading them (or by drying them which is more common throughout the world).

The most important vegetables are white cabbage (fresh or pickled which is known in Germany as *Sauerkraut*) and turnips. For the **Hungarian** cuisine sweet pepper and onions (a special, mild variety) can be added.

As far as meat is concerned, **Russians** do not have any preferences; all that can be said is that the traditional way of cooking meat is braising. Otherwise pork is the most popular meat in Eastern Europe and although you might think so, geese do not play a very important role in the Polish cuisine, they are mainly exported.

The **Slovak** cuisine has a very rich tradition of ewe's (or sheep's) cheese, and carp is a landmark in **Bohemia**.

The <u>leading alcoholic drinks</u> are in **Russia** and **Poland** *vodka*, in the **Czech Republik** *becherovka* (spirit with herbs) and beer (lager beer) and in **Slovakia** *slivovice* (spirit with plums).

Please note that Lent and Easter have a very strong tradition in **Russia** and thus are widely respected even if people are not religious. According to the Russian-Orthodox tradition, butter, dripping, eggs, milk, and of course meat, are out of the question during Lent.

Mediterranean Countries

In almost all the Mediterranean countries breakfast does not play an important role, so that the main meals of the day are lunch or dinner.

A love for <u>fresh</u> vegetables and fish and shellfish can be found all over the whole area.

Especially in **Spain** every region is proud of its own specialties, but there is a distinctive preference for olive oil, fish – cod is a favorite – and shellfish. The same is true for **Portugal**, but one difference is that the **Portuguese** seem to prefer dishes which are slightly more rich and spicy.

As the religious Orthodox tradition of fasting, which in **Greece** includes every Wednesday and Friday, is regarded by quite a lot of people (not only by religious minded people but not so much in big cities any more), meat is not allowed during this time so that vegetables are the main food for many Greeks. As far as meat is concerned they prefer meat from young animals.

International Food

Israel

As most people in this country are Jews, it can be helpful to remember that 'your' guests from these countries probably obey the Jewish dietary rules, which allow any kind of vegetables and fruits but forbid eating or drinking the following:

- haremeat, horsemeat and pork, ...
- animals living in water that do not have both fins and scales (so any kind of shellfish is forbidden), ...
- certain kinds of fowl (specifically mentioned in the Bible are e.g. hawks, owls, vultures etc.) which means that the birds you might find on our menus are usually allowed, ...
- blood (e.g. *Blutwurst* [especially as it is made of pig's blood] etc.) ...
- and the combination of meat/meat products (sausages, hamburgers etc.) with milk/milk products (butter, cheese etc.) so that for instance *Zürcher Geschnetzeltes* would be out of the question.

Of course not everyone from Israel is a religious minded person so that it can be possible that sometimes they are willing to try things they would not eat at home; but as a general rule you should keep the above in your mind, as well as the fact that people from other countries – e.g. European or American – can be Jews, too.

Islamic Countries

As most people in the **Islamic countries** – which range from **Morocco** in the West, to **Iran** in the East – are Muslims it can be helpful to remember that 'your' guests from these countries probably obey the **Islamic** dietary rules. The basic **Islamic** rules you should keep in mind are that three things are strictly forbidden: pork, blood and alcohol. Of course not everyone from these countries is a religious minded person so that it can be possible that sometimes they are willing to try things they would not eat at home; but as a general rule you should keep the above in your mind, as well as the fact that people from other countries – e.g. European or American – can be Muslims, too.

India, Southeast Asia and the Pacific Region

In the Indian cuisine there is an enormous number of vegetarian dishes and almost every dish is flavored with curry for which almost every cook in India has her or his own recipe.

Chutneys and fruits (in India this means fresh fruits) as side dishes are popular all over the country.

As a basic rule about the Indian cuisine can be said that in South India the food sometimes tends to be very hot and that there they do not eat as much lamb as in the north. A difference in cooking methods is that in the north they prefer 'dry' cooking (e.g. roasting, broiling etc.) and in the south most dishes are prepared by stewing. Although there are very many countries in the rest of this vast region there are some things that can be said in general about its cuisines:

- during history the Chinese cuisine has had a strong influence, ...
- the preferred meat is pork and chicken, ...
- the most important part of a meal is rice, ...
- ginger and chile are used to flavor almost any dish, ...
- coconuts (meat, oil, milk and sprouts which are called palm cabbage) are a basis for very many dishes ...
- and in each of the many countries the food in the southern regions is normally spicier than that in the northern regions.

Especially in **Pakistan** and **Indonesia** most of the people are Muslims so that they would obey the Islamic dietary rules (see Islamic Countries).

426822

China

The different regions in China have their own likes and dislikes, but there are a few general characteristics which can be found in Chinese cooking:

- it is only in the north of China that people use quite a lot of wheat flour; in all other regions rice is the most important corn, ...
- pork is the meat that is eaten most, ...
- chicken and duck are the favored poultry, ...
- fish is a very impotant part in the Chinese cuisine everywhere in China, ...
- bamboo shoots, bean sprouts, mushrooms and water chestnuts are preferred as vegetables ...
- and instead of salt the Chinese cooks often use soybean sauce.

What is interesting about Chinese cooking is that cooks try to have a balance between dishes of meat and of corn. Ordinary tea – green or fermented – or jasmin tea are the drinks that go with everything.

Japan

Japan has made an art of cooking fish and shellfish which – as you might well know – are sometimes eaten raw. Favorite methods of cooking them are broiling (sometimes after having been salted) or deep-frying. The preferred meat is beef but also pork or chicken. Rice is the traditional side dish, but especially when eating European food the Japanese often like bread instead of rice. Potatoes, eggplants (i.e. aubergines) and bamboo shoots are the vegetables which a Japanese guest will like; mushrooms are very popular too, but not necessarily *champignons* but the Asian variety *shiitake*, which by now are well known in Europe as well. You will never be wrong if you offer Japanese – green, i.e. not fermented – tea with a meal, whereas as an alcoholic drink they favor *sake* (made of rice).

America

It can be said that the North American cuisine of today is not very much different from the food in Europe. America has always taken over elements from other countries' cooking, so that North American guests will be used to eating all the things they find on the menu of 'your' restaurant. But please do not forget that especially in the USA there is a very strong health movement so that anything 'light', 'low-fat', 'fat free', 'low in calories' etc. may be preferred by them.

The kind of meat that is preferred in the Latin American cuisine is beef, cooked in almost any way, although frying is a very popular cooking method – especially in Mexico (this is not only true for meat but other food as well – sometimes even as a second cooking after having boiled, baked etc. the food). Corn plays a very important role everywhere in **Latin America** either as a side dish or – ground to flour – as a basis for various products.

M25

Austria-Pousse-Café

1/3 Grenadinesirup
1/3 Crème de Cacao, weiß
1/3 Cherry Brandy

Die einzelnen Zutaten werden nacheinander in der oben genannten Reihenfolge vorsichtig über den Rücken eines Barlöffels in ein Pousse-Café-Glas oder in ein Sektglas (Flöte) gegossen. Das Getränk wird mit einem Trinkhalm serviert.

Mary Pickford

1/2 weißer Rum
1/2 frischer Ananassaft
1 BL (= Barlöffel) Grenadinesirup
1 Spritzer Maraschino

Die Zutaten werden in einen Shaker mit zerstoßenem Eis gefüllt, geschüttelt und in ein vorgekühltes, doppelt großes Cocktailglas abgeseiht.

Angel Face

2 cl Dry Gin
2 cl Apricot Brandy
2 cl Calvados

Die Zutaten werden in einem Shaker mit Würfeleis geschüttelt und dann abgeseiht.

Princeton

4 cl Dry Gin
2 cl roter Portwein
2 Tropfen Orange-Bitter
1 Zitronenschale

Die Zutaten werden in einem Mixglas mit 4 bis 5 Eiswürfeln verrührt und dann in ein Cocktailglass abgeseiht. Abschließend wird die Zitronenschale über dem Cocktail ausgedrückt. Das Glas kann mit etwas Zitronenschale dekoriert werden.

Blutgeschwür-Pousse-Café

4 cl Advokaat
2 cl Cherry Brandy

Die einzelnen Zutaten werden nacheinander in der oben genannten Reihenfolge vorsichtig über den Rücken eines Barlöffels in ein Pousse-Café-Glas oder in ein Sektglas (Flöte) gegossen. Das Getränk wird mit einem Trinkhalm serviert.

Affinity

1/4 Vermouth dry
1/4 Vermouth rosso
1/2 Scotch Whisky

Die Zutaten werden in der genannten Reihenfolge in ein Mixglas mit Eiswürfeln gegeben, durchgerührt und abgeseiht.

426824

M26

1
2
3
4
5
6
7
8
9
10
11
12
13
14
15
16
17
18
19
20
21
22
23
24
25
26
27
28
29
30
1,5%
3,5%
JELLY
DECAFFEINAT

M27

1
2
3
4
5
6
7
8
9
10
11
12
13
14
15
16
17
18
19
20

M28

The Alto Motel
Gatlinburg, Tennessee

Alto is three minutes walk from the Gatlinburg Civic Auditorium, five from downtown Gatlinburg and five from Mynatt Park, with its lighted tennis courts, picnic and playground areas, as well as public basketball and baseball.

Alto is also just a few steps from a miniature golf course and the world's largest indoor theater screen at Gatlinburg Place, a mini-theme park with a whole evenings entertainment on premises.

Alto is a two minute drive from the spectacular Roaring Fork Auto Tour, a seven mile motor nature trail winding through mountain views and deep woods of the Great Smoky Mountains National Park.

Alto is within walking distance of five churches. Just take a moment to look over the map on the back of this brochure ...

Gatlinburg's Trolley, an authentic reproduction of an old-time trolley car, picks up every 15 minutes at our office door – a new way to travel around while you are in Gatlinburg.

The Alto staff takes pride in getting to know our guests and are always glad to help with travel, sight-seeing, or restaurant tips. You'll never get the brushoff at our front desk!

Alto has available loaner alarm clock, rollaways, and cribs, as well as inroom cable tv and movie channels 8 and 11.

All rooms are equipped with combination tub and shower, individual heat and air, adjacent parking, and wheelchair ramps. Each room is equipped with cube refrigerator and dial-through phones.

Alto offers swings, picnic area and an oversize pool. Ice is free and soft drinks are less than at many area markets.

Alto has peace and quiet, no saturday night only guests or youth groups. We care about your rest time.

Try us this trip. Most people come back again and again!

The Lancaster Hotel

Houston, Texas

The Lancaster, located in the heart of Houston's cultural and business center, features 93 beautifully furnished rooms and suites which engender a traditional warmth and personality, yet cater to the demanding needs of today's business traveller. Special services include complimentary limousine within the business district, full health facilities, valet, concierge, and 24-hour room service. Guest rooms feature two-line speaker telephones with facsimile and personal computer capability, minibars, robes, and Italian marble bathrooms with brass appointments.

The Lancaster grill offers the finest in Continental and American cuisine, serving breakfast, lunch, dinner, and pre- and post-theater fare. Three private meeting rooms provide the perfect setting for board meetings and intimate social gatherings.

The Lancaster is conveniently located downtown, in the heart of Houston's Financial and Theater Districts.

426826

M29

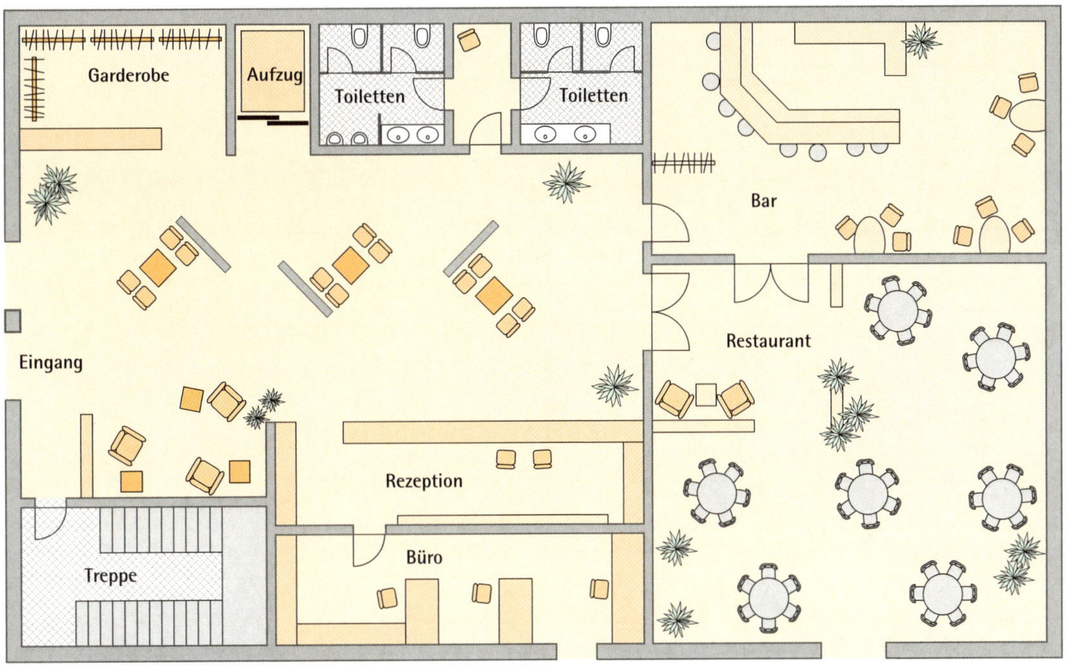
Garderobe
Aufzug
Toiletten
Toiletten
Bar
Eingang
Restaurant
Rezeption
Treppe
Büro

M30

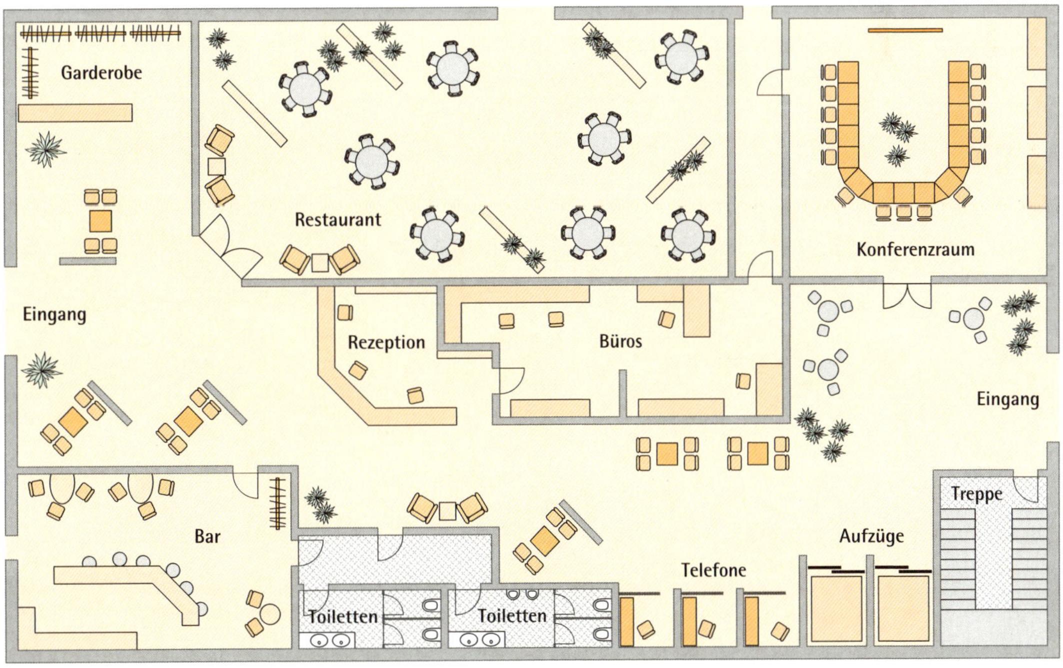
Garderobe
Restaurant
Konferenzraum
Eingang
Rezeption
Büros
Eingang
Bar
Treppe
Aufzüge
Telefone
Toiletten
Toiletten

M31

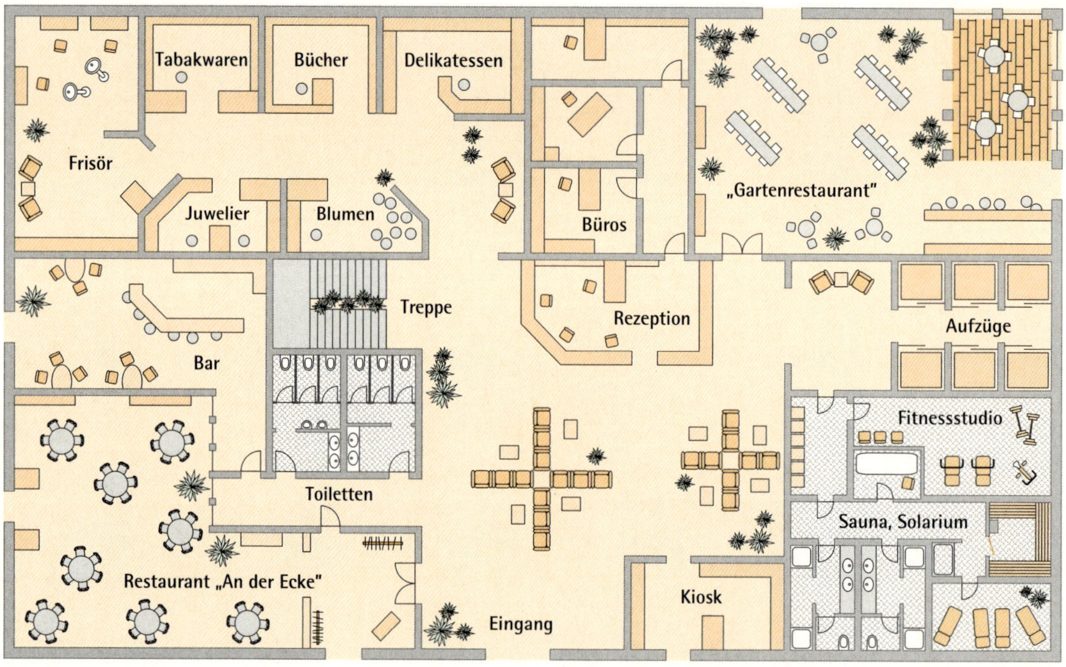

M32

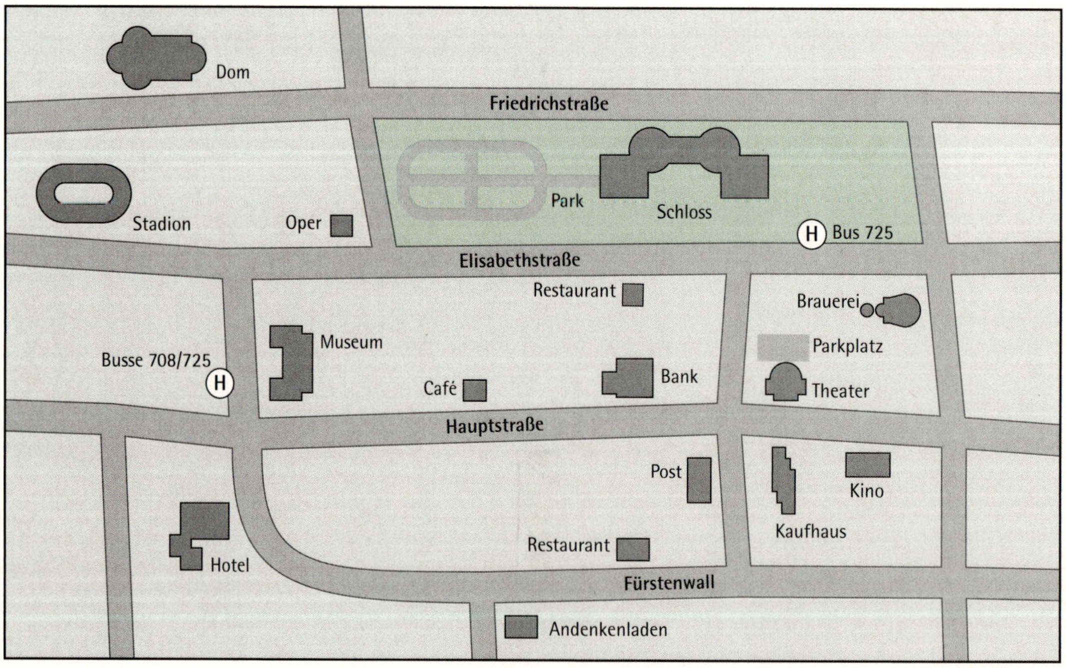

426828

Complaints and Special Wishes in the Hotel

M33

M34

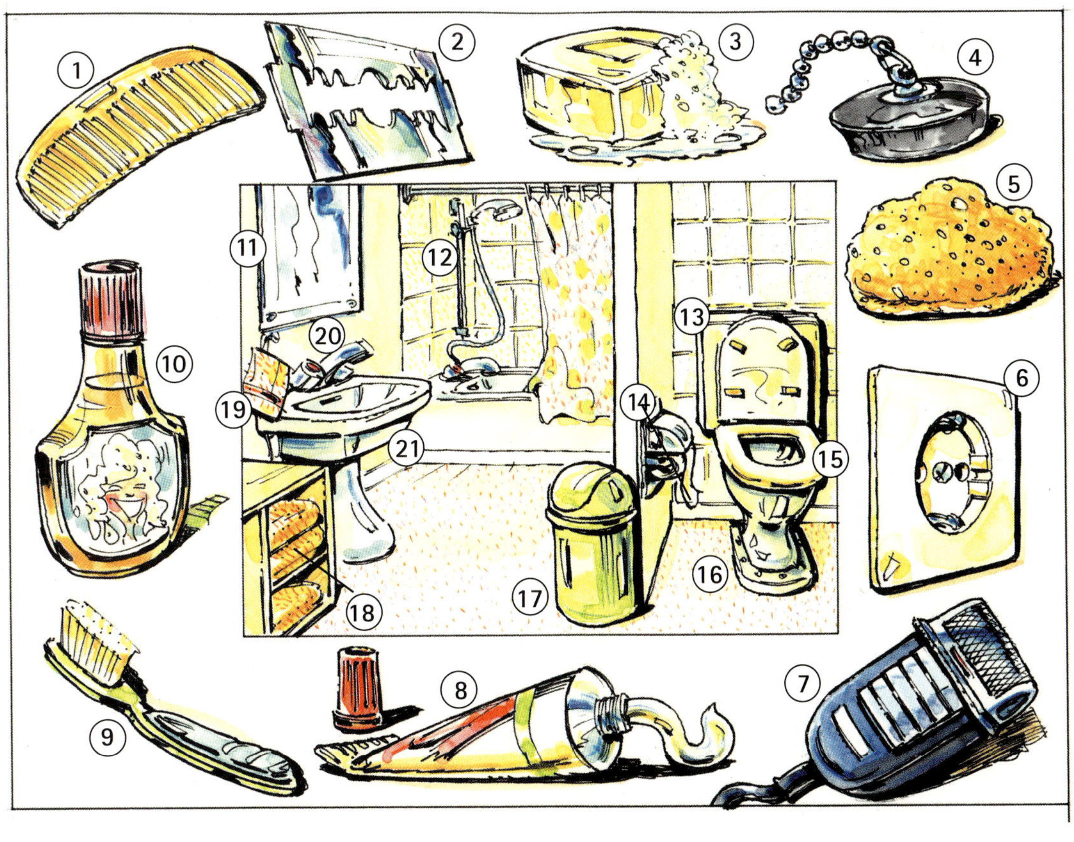

M35

Hier sind einige Merkpunkte für die Abfassung von englischsprachiger Geschäftskorrespondenz.

Liegt kein gedruckter Briefkopf vor, steht der **Absender** rechts oben.

Die **reference intitials** bestehen entweder aus einem Aktenzeichen oder den Initialen der/des für den Brief Verantwortlichen (im folgenden Brief: Nathaniel Bumppo, Chairman) sowie der Briefeschreiberin/des Briefeschreibers (im folgenden Brief: Judith Hutter, Secretary).

Im AE können die eigenen *reference intitials* auch am Ende des Schreibens der Unterschrift folgen.

Es empfiehlt sich im **Datum** den Monat in Buchstabenform (u. U. abgekürzt) zu schreiben, um Verwechselungen zu vermeiden, da es vor allem im amerikanischen Englisch (inzwischen aber auch in GB) üblich ist, den Monat vor den Tag zu setzen: also **02-07-20..** für den **07. Februar 20..** oder nach der europäischen Norm **20..-02-07.**

Soll das Schreiben an den Inhaber einer bestimmten Position innerhalb einer Firma gehen, dessen Name jedoch unbekannt ist, wird in der **Anschrift** diese Position genannt: *The F & B Manager*
Parkstreet Hotel

Die – immer hervorgehobene – **subject line** kann auch zwischen Anrede und *body of the letter* stehen.

Die **Anrede** lautet:
- wenn die Person namentlich bekannt ist: *Dear Mrs/Miss/Mr* ..., (Komma!). Im englischen Sprachraum wird auf die Unterscheidung zwischen *Mrs* und *Miss* durchaus noch geachtet oder sogar Wert gelegt. Allerdings ist inzwischen auch die neutrale Form *Ms* ... akzeptiert.
- wenn der Name des Adressaten unbekannt ist: (AE) *Gentlemen/Ladies and Gentlemen*: (Doppelpunkt!); (BE) *Dear Madam/Sir*, (Komma!). Eine Entsprechung für das deutsche „Sehr geehrte Damen und Herren" gibt es im BE nicht; die Phrase *Dear Sirs and Mesdames*, ist eine deutsche Wortschöpfung und wird von *English native speakers* als eher lächerlich empfunden, *Dear Sir/Sirs*, jedoch als korrekt akzeptiert. Im Übrigen empfiehlt es sich bei wichtigen Briefen vorher (z. B. telefonisch) den Namen des Anzuschreibenden in Erfahrung zu bringen.

In den angelsächsischen Ländern wird relativ schnell zum Gebrauch der Vornamen übergegangen (ohne dass das mit einem plumpen Duzen verwechselt werden sollte), sodass bei längeren Briefwechseln mit Geschäftspartnern so verfahren werden kann. Im Kontakt mit Hotel- oder Restaurantgästen sollte dies jedoch vermieden werden.

Das erste Wort des **body of the letter** beginnt mit einem großen Buchstaben. Der erste Abschnitt sollte den Grund des Schreibens nennen. Im Falle von Briefen an Gäste liegt in aller Regel ein Bezug auf eine vorher erhaltene Anfrage, Reservierung o. Ä. vor. Der zweite Abschnitt enthält die relevanten Informationen (Angebot, Reservierungsbestätigung o. Ä.). Der Brief endet mit ein, zwei freundlichen Sätzen zur Verabschiedung.

→ Es sollte grundsätzlich auf einen nicht nur höflichen, sondern sogar freundlichen Ton geachtet werden. Deutsche Sprecher bzw. Schreiber des Englischen werden von *English native speakers* oftmals als brüsk oder gar schroff und somit als – ungewollt – unhöflich angesehen.

Die **Verabschiedung** wird durch ein Komma abgetrennt und lautet:
- wenn der Empfänger namentlich angeschrieben wurde (z. B. *Dear Mr Henderson*): (AE) *Sincerely yours*, (BE) *Yours sincerely*,
- wenn der Name des Adressaten unbekannt ist: (AE) meist *(Very) truly yours*, (BE) *Yours faithfully*.

Es ist üblich unter die Unterschrift den Namen und evtl. die Position der/des Unterzeichnenden zu tippen.

Mitunter wird lediglich die Anzahl der **Anlagen** genannt und keine inhaltliche Auflistung vorgenommen.

426830

M36

Leatherstocking Inc.

132 W. Lincoln Hwy.
De Kalb, IL 60115
USA

Your ref.: --/-- Our ref.: NB/jh Date: Feb. 9, 20..

Haus zur Bruchbude
Sumpfgasse 123
45678 Kleinkleckersdorf
Germany

Private rooms and conference facilities

Ladies and Gentlemen:

We have learnt from our German partner, Klömperkamp GmbH & Co. KG, that your house is the ideal place to hold a conference and to relax at the same time.

As we are planning to hold our annual meeting in Germany next year we would like to combine work with holidays. We would be most thankful, if you could make us an offer concerning a stay of 40 persons for the first two weeks in August. We are interested especially in your conference facilities and your leisure and sports facilities.
Please send us some illustrated literature and your price list.

We are looking forward to hearing from you soon.

Truly yours,

Nathaniel Bumppo
Chairman

M37

Haus zur
Bruchbude

Sumpfgasse 123
45678 Kleinkleckersdorf

Tel.: 0987-123456
Fax: 0987-654321

Your ref.: NB/jh Our ref.: MM/oo Feb. 15, 20..

Leatherstocking Inc.
Mr Nathaniel Bumppo, Chairman
132 W. Lincoln Hwy.
DE KALB, IL 60115
USA

Private rooms and conference facilities

Dear Mr Bumppo,

We thank you for your inquiry dated February 9 concerning a stay of 40 of your staff at our hotel.
For your information we are sending you our latest brochure as well as the current price list. Please, note that on conferences with at least 50 members we can grant a reduction of 15 % on our standard price.
A special offer for your company are three meals at € 155.00 p.p./p.d. (soft drinks included).
As you are especially interested in leisure facilities we would like to point out that we would be happy to arrange for your group the booking of tickets for a concert of the "Festival of Classical Music" and a gala dinner during the second week of your stay. These open air concerts have a very good reputation and are regarded as among the best in the world; we enclose this year's program and price list. This offer is valid until March 10.
We hope that we could answer all your questions. In case any further ones should arise, please do not hesitate to contact us.

Sincerely yours,

Meta Mustermann
Sales Manager

Enc.: 4

426832

M38

Leatherstocking Inc.

132 W. Lincoln Hwy.
De Kalb, IL 60115
USA

Your ref.: MM/oo   Our ref.: NB/jh   Date: March 3, 20..

Haus zur Bruchbude
Sales Department
Sumpfgasse 123
45678 Kleinkleckersdorf
Germany

Private rooms and conference facilities

Dear Mrs Mustermann,

Thank you very much for your offer dated February 15. I am glad to tell you that it fully meets our expectations so that herewith I would like to book from August 3 until August 17 the following:

– 20 single rooms	at € 85.00 p.n.
– 16 double rooms	at € 130.00 p.n.
– 1 conference room "Albrecht Dürer"	at € 235.00 p.d. (incl. 15 % discount)
– 52 tickets (Festival of Classical Music) for Saturday, August 7 including the gala dinner	at € 230.00 per ticket.

Furthermore I would like to accept your offer of 3 meals a day at € 155.00 p.p. for all members of our group for a total of 10 days.

Please confirm this booking.

We thank you for your cooperation and are looking forward to our stay in Germany.
Sincerely yours,

Nathaniel Bumppo
Chairman

M39

Haus zur
Bruchbude

Sumpfgasse 123
45678 Kleinkleckersdorf

Tel.: 0987-123456
Fax: 0987-654321

Your ref.: NB/jh Our ref.: MM/oo March 8, 20..

Leatherstocking Inc.
Mr Nathaniel Bumppo, Chairman
132 W. Lincoln Hwy.
DE KALB, IL 60115
USA

Private rooms and conference facilities

Dear Mr Bumppo,

We thank you for your booking of March 3 which we hereby confirm:

		total
from 3 to 17 August		
– 20 single rooms	at € 85.00 p.n.	€ 23,800.00
– 16 double rooms	at € 130.00 p.n.	€ 29,120.00
– 1 conference room "Albrecht Dürer"	at € 235.00 p.d.	
	(incl. 15 % discount)	€ 2,796.50
– 52 tickets (Festival of Classical Music)	at € 230.00 per ticket	€ 11,960.00
– 3 meals at € 155.00 p.p./p.d. for 10 days		€ 80,600.00
		€ 148,276.50

We would be thankful if you could inform us five days in advance of your arrival for which 10 days of your stay you would like to accept the special offer of three meals a day.
We look forward to welcoming you in August.

Sincerely yours,

Meta Mustermann
Sales Manager

426834

M40

Haus zur Bruchbude

Sumpfgasse 123
45678 Kleinkleckersdorf

Tel: 0987-123456
Fax: 0987-654321

Your ref.: NB/jh Our ref.: MM/oo Oct. 1, 20..

Leatherstocking Inc.
Mr Nathaniel Bumppo, Chairman
132 W. Lincoln Hwy.
DE KALB, IL 60115
USA

Private rooms and conference facilities

Dear Mr Bumppo,

May we draw your attention to the fact that you seem to have overlooked your overdue account of € 148,276.50 for the stay of 52 staff of your company at our hotel in the time from August 3 until August 17 (see our invoice # 08/15 of August 17)?

Please see to this matter and let us have your remittance in the near future.

If you have settled the amount in the meantime, please disregard this communication.

Sincerely yours,

Meta Mustermann
Sales Manager

M41

THE PARENTICIDE CLUB

138 W. Lincoln Hwy.
De Kalb
IL 60115

Your Ref.: MM/-- Our ref.: AGB/sc Nov. 24, 20..

Haus zur Bruchbude
Mrs Meta Mustermann, Sales Manager
Sumpfgasse 123
45678 Kleinkleckersdorf
Germany

Private rooms and conference facilities

Dear Mrs Mustermann,

We hear from “Leatherstocking, Inc.” that your house is the ideal place to work in a relaxing and comfortable atmosphere.
As we are planning to have some very important talks with representatives of our German twin clubs, we would be most thankful, if you could make us an offer concerning a stay of a team of eight persons (single rooms, please) for the last three weeks in May next year. For the first two weeks of that period we would also need a conference room for about 15 people, which provides a very private atmosphere. During the last week of our stay we would like to take the opportunity to get to know a little bit more about your lovely country, as none of us has ever stayed in Germany before.

We should appreciate your early reply.

Sincerely yours,

Ambrose G. Bierce
President

426836

M42

Haus zur
Bruchbude

Sumpfgasse 123
45678 Kleinkleckersdorf

Tel: 0987-123456
Fax: 0987-654321

Your ref.: AGB/sc   Our ref.: MM/oo   Dec. 6, 20..

The Parenticide Club
Mr Ambrose Bierce, President
138 W. Lincoln Hwy.
DE KALB, IL 60115
USA

Private rooms and conference facilities

Dear Mr Bierce,

We thank you very much for your inquiry dated November 24. As we are fully booked at the time in question, however, we regret that we have to inform you that we are in no position whatsoever to carry out any booking for the "Parenticide Club" during this time.

May we point out that we would be happy to reserve the required rooms for you any time from June 21 until the end of August. We enclose our hotel brochure and price list as well as some information about special summer activities we offer during that time.

We trust that our situation finds your kind understanding and look forward to carry out any booking for you should you alter your plans.

Sincerely yours,

Meta Mustermann
Sales Manager

Encl.: 4

M43

Grundsätzlich gelten für das Layout eines Bewerbungsschreibens die gleichen Kriterien wie für die übrige Geschäftskorrespondenz (vgl. S. 30).

> Hier sind einige Merkpunkte für die Abfassung von englischsprachigen Bewerbungen.

Zusätzlich sollte bei dem *covering letter* noch auf Folgendes geachtet werden:

- Führen Sie aus, was Sie veranlasst hat den Brief zu schreiben (z. B. Anzeige, persönliche Information usw.).
- Weisen Sie auf Besonderheiten hin, die in der Kürze des beigefügten Lebenslaufs nicht deutlich werden. Vermeiden Sie es aber auf alle Fälle, die Stichpunkte des Lebenslaufs lediglich im Volltext zu wiederholen.
- Haben Sie keine Hemmungen, Ihre Fähigkeiten und Qualitäten zu betonen („Klappern gehört zum Handwerk."), tragen Sie aber nicht zu dick auf und erwähnen Sie nichts Negatives (z. B. eine Prüfung beim ersten Versuch nicht bestanden). Negatives im Bewerbungsschreiben verringert Ihre Chancen zu einem Gespräch geladen zu werden (in dem es dann u. U. angesprochen werden kann).

M44

Als Reaktion auf die nebenstehende Anzeige erhält der Personalchef des Hotels Vasa den folgenden Brief.

STADSHOTELLET VASA

Applications are invited for the position of a

DEPUTY HEAD WAITRESS/WAITER

The applicant is required
to assist the head waiter
and in his absence to perform his duties.

A minimum of three years' experience
in restaurant work at first class restaurants is essential.

Please apply in writing to:

Walter S. Scott
Human Resources Officer
Stadtshotellet Vasa
Kungsgatan 34
65108 Karlstad
Sweden

Als Anlagen sind dem Brief der Lebenslauf, ein Referenzgutachten des Ausbildungshotels sowie das Oberstufenhalbjahreszeugnis der Berufsschule beigefügt.

426838

M45

Adelheid von Walldorf
Goethestraße 23
40237 Düsseldorf

Tel.: +49 211 1234567
Fax: +49 211 7654321

20..-02-14

Walter S. Scott – Human Resources Officer
Stadtshotellet Vasa
Kungsgatan 34
65108 KARLSTAD
SWEDEN

Advertisement in "Caterer & Hotelkeeper" of Feb. 8, 20..
for the post of a deputy head waitress/head waiter

Dear Mr Scott,

I am writing to apply for the position of deputy head waitress which you advertised in last week's issue of "Caterer & Hotelkeeper".

As you can see from my CV I am currently undergoing training – until July – as a waitress at the five-star "Hotel Grafenburg" in Düsseldorf. In the three years of my training I was able to gather a considerable amount of experience in restaurant service as the hotel's head waiter could not perform his job because of a serious illness for a period of 10 months during which time I was allowed to take over his responsibilities. That I was able to do so to the complete satisfaction of my employers you can see from the testimonial I enclose.
Please let me point out in this context that the training in Germany is organized in a dual system: I work at the hotel where I get my practical experience and once a week I go to a technical college where theoretical background knowledge is taught.
As my employer is in no position to offer me a permanent job after my final exams I would like to take the opportunity to develop my professional skills in a first class establishment abroad. Having spent my vacation in Sweden fairly regularly I developed a love for your beautiful country. I am currently attending a course in Swedish.

I am positive that my qualifications meet with your expectations.

I look forward to hearing from you soon.

Sincerely yours,

Adelheid von Walldorf

Encl.: 3

M46

Curriculum Vitae

Adelheid von Walldorf	Name
Goethestraße 23 40237 Düsseldorf	Address
+49 211 1234567	Telephone
+49 211 7654321	Telefax
20 April, 1982	Date of Birth
Düsseldorf	Place of Birth
German	Nationality

Education

Training as *Hotelfachfrau* (hotel and catering student) • at „Hotel Grafenburg“ in Düsseldorf • at „Albrecht-Dürer-Schule“ in Düsseldorf (technical college)	August 2001 – July 2004
Abitur (higher education entrance qualification) • Subjects: English, Social Science • Grade 1.9 (out of 6: 1 = very good; 6 = extremely inadequate)	May 2001

Qualifications

• French (ambilingual) • English (fluent) • Swedish (working knowledge)	Languages
• Windows XP/NT • Word/Excel • Fidelio	Computer Skills
• soccer (Swedish and German leagues) • cooking • parachuting	Interests

426840

M47

Wenn Sie nicht sicher sind, ob im Land Ihrer Wahl das duale Ausbildungssystem bekannt ist, sollten Sie es (am besten im *covering letter*) kurz umreißen, da sonst u. U. davon ausgegangen wird, dass Sie kaum praktische Berufserfahrung besitzen.

Da es keine genauen englischsprachigen Entsprechungen für deutsche Schularten, -stufen und -abschlüsse gibt, empfiehlt es sich, im *CV* bzw. im *covering letter* die deutschen Begriffe zu verwenden. In Klammern kann dann ein erklärender Zusatz aus der Terminologie des Landes, für das man sich bewirbt, folgen: z. B. in einem Brief nach GB *„Abitur equiv. (= equivalent) to A-Level"*.

Im Folgenden finden Sie einige englischsprachige Entsprechungen zu deutschen Begriffen:

Internat	–	*boarding school*
Gesamtschule	–	*comprehensive school*
Hauptschule	–	*secondary general school*
Realschule	–	*intermediate (secondary) school*
Gymnasium	–	*grammar school*
Handelsschule/HöHa	–	*two year pre-vocational commercial course*
Fachoberschule	–	*secondary technical school*
Berufsschule	–	*technical college*

Fachoberschulreife	–	*secondary technical school entrance qualification*
Abitur	–	*higher education entrance qualification*
Abschluss (Berufsschul~)	–	*leaving certificate (technical college leaving certificate)*
Berufsabschluss	–	*vocational qualification*

Teilzeitunterricht	–	*day release course*
Blockunterricht	–	*block release course*

Ausbildung	–	*training* (*apprenticeship* wird im Englischen lediglich für eine Ausbildung im Handwerk benutzt)
Praktikum	–	*work placement*

Hotelfachfrau/-mann	–	*fully qualified graduate in the hotel and catering business*
Restaurantfachfrau/-mann	–	*fully qualified waitress/waiter*
Köchin/Koch	–	*fully qualified chef*

M48

Englische Übersetzungen deutscher Berufsbegriffe sind immer sehr schwierig, da die Tätigkeitsbereiche oftmals nicht identisch sind bzw. sich überlappen. Selbst innerhalb des deutschsprachigen Raums werden von Hotel zu Hotel mit den gleichen Begriffen mitunter nicht deckungsgleiche Verantwortungsbereiche umschrieben (ganz abgesehen davon, dass gerade in dieser Branche oftmals englische Begriffe benutzt werden, die jedoch rein deutsche Wortschöpfungen sind – z. B. **stewarding, *night auditing*). Deshalb scheint es günstiger, Ihre Erfahrungen und bisherigen Tätigkeiten zu **beschreiben**. Im Folgenden bieten wir zu Ihrer Hilfe einige Phrasen und Begriffe *(activities, departments, staff)*, um Tätigkeitsbereiche zu beschreiben:

- *to be responsible for ...* — *I was responsible for seeing after the laundry.*
- *to be in charge of ...* — *I was in charge of all the stores of the hotel.*
- *to supervise* — *It was my office to supervise the cleaning staff.*
- *to work with ...* — *I worked with the cleaning staff.*
- *to work in ...* — *I worked in the sales department.*
- *to work as ...* — *I worked as a receptionist ...*
- *to include* — *... which included answering all incoming telephone calls.*

Departments		Staff
		manager (e.g. *f&b manager*) head of staff (e.g. *head receptionist*) assistant (e.g. *assistant f&b manager*) deputy *(deputy head receptionist)*
administration	sales office	accountant
	human resources office, staff office, (esp. BE) personnel office	human resources officer, staff manager, (esp. BE) personnel manager
food and beverage department	kitchen restaurant bar banqueting	chef waitress, waiter bartender, (BE) barman
front office	reception	receptionist, cashier, porter
	reservation office	(switchboard) operator, (BE) telephonist
housekeeping department	housekeeping	housekeeper, chambermaid, cleaning staff
	stores	storekeeper
	maintenance	technician
	laundry department	

M49

POPPER'S PUDDINGS LTD.

MANUFACTURERS OF
TRADITIONAL HIGH QUALITY FOODS
SINCE 1878

are looking for a

Sales Manager

to be responsible for the continual sales development in the Edinburgh area. Management experience and driving license mandatory. Salary negotiable.

Please apply in writing to:

Peter Popper, Sales Director
Popper's Puddings Ltd.
101 Southwark Street
London SE1 0JH

THE STAFFORD
St. James's Place
London SW1A 1NJ
Great Britain

- first class restaurant with classic English and French cuisine
- famous 350 year old wine cellar
- furnished with an understated elegance
- single rooms at £184
  double/twin rooms at £200-215
  suites at £253-430
- direct access to Green Park
- very near Buckingham Palace and St. James's Park

The
MANSON ON TURTLE CREEK
2821 Turtle Creek Blvd.
Dallas
Texas 75219
USA

- 1925 Italian Renaissance Style residence
- first class award winning restaurant
- close to the Dallas business and arts districts
- rooms and suites with marble baths
- 5 min. from downtown Dallas / 25 min. from DFW Int. Airport and 5 min. from Dallas Love Field

---

The
VILLA VERA HOTEL
AND RACQUET CLUB

will be requiring a

Front of House Manager

commencing February 20..

to assume full responsibilty for the day to day management of our Reception, Reservation and Sales Department.

The ideal candidate will be expected to have hotel experience in general and specialist knowledge of the front office in particular.

This position requires advanced management skills, the ability to train and motivate staff and an obsessional commitment to maximize room occupancy.

This is a senior position reporting directly to the proprietors of the hotel.

If you feel you have the right qualifications and experience please write with full CV, recent snapshot and salary expectations to:

The Proprietors / Villa Vera Hotel
Lomas del Mar # 35 / Acapulco, Gro., México

M50

Numbers – Zahlen	Deutsch	English
	Million	million
	Milliarde	billion
	Billion	trillion
	Billiarde	quadrillion

M51

Liquids – Flüssigkeiten	USA		metric			metrisch		USA
	gallon		pint		liter	Liter		Pint
			1 pt		0,47 l	1 l	≈	2.11 pt
	1 gall	=	8 pt	≈	3,78 l			

M52

Liquids – Flüssigkeiten	GB				metric	metrisch	GB
	gallon		pint		litre	Liter	pint
			1 pt	≈	0,57 l	1 l	1.76 pt
	1 gall	=	8 pt	≈	4,54 l		

Inzwischen stellt man in **Großbritannnien** auf das metrische System um. Getränke (Milch, Säfte usw.) werden z. B. in Supermärkten auch in Liter- bzw. Halbliterpackungen und -flaschen verkauft. Benzin wird ebenfalls nur noch in Litern abgegeben. In *Pubs*, Bars, Restaurants u. Ä. dürfen Spirituosen nur noch in cl ausgeschenkt werden: 2 cl entsprechen ungefähr *7.04 fluid ounces (fl oz)*.

M53

Weights	USA/GB					metric
	stone		pound		gram	kilogram
			1 lb	≈	454 gr	
	1 st	=	14 lb		≈	6,36 kg

M54

Gewichte	metrisch					USA/GB		
	Kilogramm		Pfund		Gramm		pound/stone
			1 Pfund	=	500 g	≈	1.10 lb
	1 kg	=	2 Pfund	–	1 000 g	≈	0.16 st

M55

Temperature – Temperatur	Fahrenheit		Celsius	Celsius		Fahrenheit
	100°	≈	38°	35°	≈	95°
	90°	≈	32°	30°	≈	86°
	80°	≈	27°	25°	≈	77°
	70°	≈	21°	20°	≈	68°
	60°	≈	16°	15°	≈	59°
	50°	≈	10°	10°	≈	50°
	40°	≈	4°	5°	≈	41°
	30°	≈	–1°	0°	≈	32°
	20°	≈	–7°	–5°	≈	23°
	10°	≈	–12°	–10°	≈	14°
	0°	≈	–8°	–15°	≈	5°

Degrees Centigrade = Degrees Celsius

Offiziell gilt sowohl in den USA als auch in GB die Celsiusskala. Doch wird im allgemeinen Sprachgebrauch nach wie vor immer noch häufig Fahrenheit benutzt. Wetterberichte u. Ä. geben meistens beide Temperatureinheiten an. Im wissenschaftlichen Sprachgebrauch wird ausschließlich Celsius benutzt.

M56

Distance/Length	USA/GB								metric
	mile		yard		foot		inch		centimeter/meter/ kilometer
							1 in	≈	2,54 cm
					1 ft	=	12 in	≈	30,47 cm
			1 yd	=	3 ft	=	36 in	≈	91,40 cm
			100 yds					≈	91,40 m
	1 mile	=	1760 yds					≈	1,61 km

M57

Entfernungs- und Längenmaße	metrisch		USA/GB						
	Zentimeter/ Meter/ Kilometer		inch		foot		yard		mile
	1 cm	≈	0.39 in						
	1 m	≈	39.39 in	≈	3.28 ft	≈	1.09 yds		
	100 m			≈	328.23 ft	≈	109.41 yds		
	1 km					≈	1094.09 yds	≈	0.62 miles

Das Standard-Hotelbett in Deutschland (200 cm) ist somit ungefähr *6 feet 7 inches (6' 7")* lang; gesagt wird in aller Regel *six foot seven* oder – seltener – *six feet seven* (ohne *inches*!).

426846

M58

When guests from abroad are in Germany they most probably want to try German food – at least that's what you would expect. Nevertheless you ought to be prepared in case international guests of 'your' restaurant or hotel are reluctant to try German food, whatever their reasons may be. The farther away from Central Europe a guest's home country the more different is her or his culture and – consequently – the more different is the food she or he is used to; religious rules (see below), which prescribe or forbid certain things, may add further complications.

So it might prove quite helpful to have at least some basic ideas about several national cuisines and thus about the things a guest may be used to and may favor as her or his diet. Your recommendations can be based on this knowledge and guests who may have inhibitions about trying foreign food most certainly will thank you for your considerateness.

There are quite a lot of **Religious Dietary Rules** which many – though certainly not all – members of a specific religion observe. Some of these rules can help to explain why, for example, a particular kind of meat is not eaten in certain regions of the world. The religions you most probably may come into contact with when working in a hotel in Central Europe are Islam, Judaism and the religions of India and East Asia (i.e. Buddhism, Hinduism, Shintoism, Sikhism ...). As the dietary rules of the latter have been very much influenced in the course of history by a very complex caste system, it is almost impossible to give a short description of these rules. So maybe the best thing you can do in case you realize that guests are not sure if they are allowed to eat a certain dish, politely ask them. The basic **Islamic** rules you ought to keep in mind are that three things are strictly forbidden: pork, blood and alcohol. The **Jewish** religion allows any kind of vegetables and fruits but forbids the consumption of the following: a) haremeat, horsemeat and pork, b) animals living in water that do not have both fins and scales (so any kind of shellfish is prohibited), c) certain kinds of fowl (specifically mentioned in the Bible are e.g. hawks, owls, vultures etc.) which means that those birds you might expect to find on our menus are basically allowed, d) blood (e.g. *Blutwurst* [especially as it is made of pig's blood] etc.) and e) the combination of meat/meat products (sausages, hamburgers etc.) with milk/milk products (butter, cheese etc.) so that for instance *Zürcher Geschnetzeltes* would be out of the question.

You will notice that in the following we do not say anything about the French and the Italian cuisines. We think that in Central Europe these two national kitchens are so well known that telling especially you – i.e. people from the hotel and catering business – about them would be like carrying coals to Newcastle.

International Food

Great Britain & Ireland

The most famous items of the cuisine in the United Kingdom are obviously 'English Breakfast' and 'Five O'Clock Tea'.

Breakfast consists not just – as you know it from the "Continental Breakfast" served in hotels – of rolls, jam and maybe some cold cuts or cheese but is almost a three-course-meal. It begins with some cereals: traditionally porridge (i.e. oatmeal boiled in milk or water) but nowadays almost always replaced by some modern variety like cornflakes, rice crispies etc. This cereal-course is followed by a mixed grill which can be comprised of almost anything that can be fried or grilled: fried or scrambled eggs, bacon, beef or pork sausages, grilled tomatoes, baked beans, mushrooms etc. Kidneys and kippers (cured herrings) have gone out of fashion nowadays. Toast with marmalade or jam concludes the breakfast. Tea or coffee are the drinks that go with this meal. The above can of course be complemented by anything you like: fruit, fruit or vegetable juices; steak or fried potatoes for the mixed grill; honey, chocolate spread and ... and ... and ...

Tea – which does not have to be served exactly at five o'clock – is not to be confused with what we call in German *Kaffeeklatsch*, "tea" is a substantial meal in itself. As the very good breakfast in the morning kept the Britons running through lunchtime right into the afternoon, lunch never was regarded as an important meal. As a consequence they were hungry again in the afternoon so that about that time it was high time for some calories. What you get nowadays when you order 'tea' in a hotel is a kind of 'three course meal': sandwiches (with cucumbers, watercress, anchovy-paste ...), scones (with butter or – more typical – with clotted cream and fruit preserve, i.e. jam), cake(s) and of course a pot of tea or coffee. 'High Tea' in the north of England and Scotland has even more courses: in addition to the above they eat fish, meat, puddings, desserts etc.

The Britons do not eat so much pork but beef and mutton or lamb. As a rule vegetables are only boiled and served without a sauce. The preferred meat in Ireland is mutton and potatoes come with everything.

A very popular item in Great Britain as well as in Ireland are puddings: dishes cooked in a mould. There is almost no limit to the variety of puddings you can find on these islands: steak and kidney pudding, black pudding (which we call *Blutwurst*), Yorkshire pudding, rice pudding, plum pudding (strangely enough you will search in vain for plums in it). Almost the same recipes are used for making pies which are more or less puddings covered by pastry.

Fish – cooked in a lot of different ways – is very popular as well among both peoples.

Scandinavia

The most prominent items of the Scandinavian cuisine are, of course, fish and shellfish which are done in inummerable ways: hot or cold, cooked or just marinaded or smoked – but never raw as you may know it from the Japanese kitchen. However, the type of fish that is preferred differs from country to country: in **Norway** it is salmon and cod, in **Sweden** it is herring. The **Danes** surprisingly do not eat so much fish – they export most of what they catch; this is why in **Denmark** a big amount of pork is consumed.

Depending on the season **Danish, Norwegian** or **Swedish** guests would be delighted if you would offer them venison as it plays an important role in their kitchen as well.

If Scandinavian guests are reluctant to try German food it may very well be that they are in favor of open sandwiches (called *smørrebrød* in **Danish** and *smorbrod* in **Norwegian**): in Scandinavia they are mostly on the basis of rye bread to which almost anything can be added – first of all, naturally, fish.

Eastern Europe

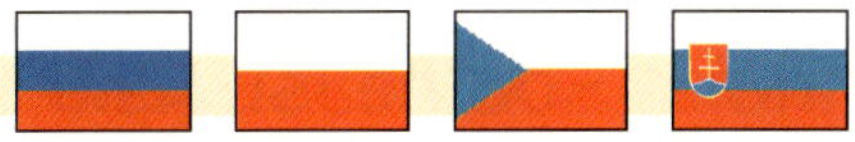

What plays a very important role in a **Russian** meal with several courses is a variety of *sakuski*, i.e. appetizers, which are mainly composed of fish, meat, eggs, marinaded or pickled vegetables and of course bread. There are absolutely no limits to your imagination as to how these can be prepared, arranged and combined.

In **Russia** soups, almost always purely vegetarian meals (or with fish), have been developed to a very nourishing standard on the one hand, on the other hand they can be very sophisticated affairs as a second course after the *sakuski*.

Considering Eastern Europe's geographical and topographical features it cannot be surprising that mushrooms are a genuine part of those countries' cuisines: in the early fall of course they are eaten fresh, right out of the vast forests. **Russia** is the only country that has developed a tradition of preserving mushrooms by marinading them (or by drying them which is more common throughout the world).

The dominating vegetables are white cabbage (fresh or pickled which is known in Germany as *Sauerkraut*) and turnips. For the **Hungarian** cuisine sweet pepper and onions (a special, mild variety) can be added to this list.

As far as meat is concerned **Russians** do not have any preferences; all that can be said is that the traditional way of cooking meat is braising. Otherwise pork is the most popular meat in Eastern Europe and although the general opinion might think so, geese do not play a very important role in the Polish cuisine, they are bred mainly to be exported.

The **Slovak** cuisine has a very rich tradition of ewe's (or sheep's) cheese and carp is a landmark in **Bohemia**.

The leading alcoholic drinks are in **Russia** and **Poland** *vodka*, in the **Czech Republik** *becherovka* (spirit with herbs) and beer (lager beer) and in **Slovakia** *slivovice* (spirit with plums).

Please note that Lent and Easter have a very strong tradition in **Russia** and thus are widely respected even if people are not religious minded. According to the Russian-Orthodox tradition butter, dripping, eggs, milk, and of course meat are out of the question during Lent.

Mediterranean Countries

As a rule breakfast does not play an important role for people in these countries, and a love for fresh vegetables on the one hand and for fish and shellfish on the other hand is what they share as well.

As the religious Orthodox tradition of fasting, which in **Greece** includes every Wednesday and Friday, is regarded by quite a lot of people (not only by religious minded people but not so much in big cities any more), meat is not allowed during this time so that vegetables are a staple diet for many Greeks. As far as meat is concerned they prefer meat from young and not so much from grown up animals; and a love of fish and shellfish is again what Greece has in common with the other Mediterranean countries.

Although it is very difficult to find any general rules applying to both countries on the Iberian Peninsula – particularly in **Spain** every region is proud of its own specialties – one thing is certain: what both countries' cuisines share is a preference for olive oil, fish – cod appears to be a favorite – and shellfish. One difference if any is that the Portuguese seem to prefer dishes which are slightly more rich and spicy.

India, Southeast Asia and the Pacific Region

Two facts are well known in Central Europe about the **Indian** cuisine: that **India** has brought forth an enormous variety of vegetarian dishes and that virtually any dish is flavored with curry for which almost every cook in India has her or his own recipe.

Fruits – in **India** this means <u>fresh</u> fruits – as side dishes are popular all over the country as well as chutneys.

Regional differences in this big country are too many to be mentioned here in detail. But a basic rule is that in South India the food sometimes tends to be very hot and that there they do not eat as much lamb as in the north. A difference in cooking methods is that in the north they prefer 'dry' cooking (e.g. roasting, broiling etc.) and in the south most dishes are prepared by way of stewing.

Vast as the area of **Southeast Asia and the Pacific Region** may seem there are some things that can be said in general about its cuisines:

- throughout history the Chinese cooking has had a strong influence, ...
- the preferred meat is pork and chicken, ...
- the meals are dominated by rice, ...
- ginger and chile are used to flavour almost any dish, ...
- coconuts (meat, oil, milk and sprouts, which are called palm cabbage) are a basis for a huge variety of dishes ...
- and the somewhat surprising fact that in each of the many countries the food in the southern regions tends to be spicier than that in the northern regions (it is common to offer condiments seperately so that the guests can use them individiually according to their tastes).

The vital factor of any **Indonesian** dish is rice *(nasi)* around which all the other elements are composed so that meat, vegetables, herbs, spices and even drinks are only supplements to rice. Well known – even in Germany – is *nasi goreng*.

The **Philippine** cooking has been influenced very much by the Spaniards; otherwise the combination of sour and salty is a striking factor about that country's food.

As **Vietnam** has a very long coast it cannot be surprising that fish is a high-ranking element in its recipes. Here the Chinese cooking has left its most prominent marks.

China

Although culinary China can be divided into five regions *(Chekiang-Kiangsu, Beijing, Szechwan*, and the less important *Fukien* and *Kwangtung*), which have their own likes and dislikes, there are a couple of general characteristics which can be found in all five schools of Chinese cooking:

- it is only in the north of China that people use quite a lot of wheat flour; in all other regions rice is the dominating corn, ...
- pork is the prevailing meat, ...
- chicken and duck are the favored poultry, ...
- fish plays a very prominent part in the Chinese cuisine no matter where in China, ...
- bamboo shoots, bean sprouts, mushrooms and water chestnuts are preferred as vegetables
- and instead of salt they use soybean sauce.

A distinguishing factor in Chinese meals or even only in a Chinese dish is that chefs – any cooks in fact – aim at counterbalancing corn on the one hand with meat and vegetables on the other hand.

Although in Central China (i.e. *Szechwan*) quite a lot of hot peppers are used the dishes cannot be called hot because they are flavored in a way that very soon this first sensation is replaced especially by that of a combination of sweet and sour.

Especially guests coming from *Chekiang* and *Kiangsu* will appreciate a decorative presentation of the food as this is the favored way of serving meals in these regions. Ordinary tea – as in Japan green or fermented – or jasmin tea are the drinks that go with everything.

Japan

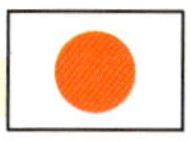

Being an island – several islands in fact – Japan has made an art of cooking fish and seafood which – as you might well know – are sometimes eaten raw. Favorite methods of cooking them are broiling (sometimes after having been salted) or deep-frying. The preferred meat is beef which can be replaced by pork or chicken. Rice is the traditional side dish, but especially when eating European food the Japanese have developed a liking for bread as a substitute for it.

Potatoes, eggplants (i.e. aubergines) and bamboo shoots are the vegetables which will find a Japanese guest's approval; mushrooms are very popular too, not necessarily *champignons* but the Asian variety *shiitake*, which by now are well known in Europe as well.

You will never be wrong if you offer Japanese – green – tea as an accompaniment to a meal, whereas as an alcoholic drink they favor *sake* (made of rice).

America

As a rule it can be said that the **North American** cuisine of today does not differ from food eaten in Europe. Being a melting pot of all the other cultures in the world America has passed on its tendency to assimilate anything into its cuisine as well, so that your **North American** guests will be used to eating all the things they are likely to find on the menu of 'your' restaurant. But please bear in mind that especially in the **USA** there is a very strong health movement so that anything 'light', 'low-fat', 'fat free', 'low in calories' etc. may be approved of by your guests.

The kind of meat that is preferred in the **Latin American** kitchen is beef, cooked in almost any way, although frying is a very popular cooking method – especially in **Mexico** (this is true not only as regards meat but other food as well – sometimes even as a second cooking after having boiled, baked etc. the food). Corn plays a very important role throughout **Latin America** either as a side dish or – ground to flour – as a basis for various products.

Describing the Restaurant

Ein Gast möchte telefonisch einen Tisch bestellen. Doch bevor er die Reservierung festmacht, hat er einige Fragen zu „Ihrem" Restaurant.

1 Beantworten Sie sich nun bitte gegenseitig diese Fragen.

What type of restaurant is it?	It's a	first class restaurant two star restaurant traditional restaurant international restaurant

Where is the restaurant?	It's	in the center on the outskirts	of the town/city of (Düsseldorf)
		in the country near the airport/station/...	

How can you get there?	It's (only)	ten minutes	by bus by car on foot	from the airport ...

What are the surroundings like?	It's	very close to not far from next to near/in	the a	center quiet area park ...

What is the interior like?	It's a	very quite	elegant modern old fashioned cozy

What is the food like?	We offer We have	international modern regional traditional	food cooking cuisine

426852

2

Versuchen Sie nun bitte „Ihr" Restaurant zusammenhängend zu beschreiben. Sie können sich zunächst Notizen machen, die Sie anschließend in einen Text umsetzen.

Zuvor ein Beispiel:

Type of restaurant:	one star restaurant; traditional, regional cooking
Seats:	84 seats, 3 rooms
Interior:	water mill, old fashioned, elegant, cozy
Where:	in the center, 5 minutes on foot from business center, 5 minutes on foot from shopping area

Gast: Can you give me some information about your restaurant, Miss?

Telefonistin: Well, madam, our restaurant is a one star restaurant with traditional regional cooking on a very high level. It is in an old water mill and offers 84 seats in 3 old fashioned but elegant and cozy rooms. It's directly in the center of Düsseldorf, only 5 minutes on foot from the main shopping area and the business center.

Nun „Ihr" Restaurant:

Type of restaurant: ______________________________

Seats: ______________________________

Interior: ______________________________

____

____

____

____

Where: ______________________________

____

____

____

____

Dealing with Guests in the Restaurant

3

Bitte lesen Sie diesen Dialog.

Dieser Dialog findet gegen Abend in einem Hotel statt. Ein Gast betritt das Restaurant.

Bedienung:	Good evening, sir. Can I help you?
Gast:	Good evening. I booked a table for one.
Bedienung:	Can you tell me your name, please?
Gast:	Sure, I'm Mr Smith. John Smith.
Bedienung:	Really?!?
Gast:	Yes, that really is my name, I'm sorry to say.
Bedienung:	Well, sir, let me see. Yes, we reserved table # 8 for you. Would you follow me to your table, please?

Einige Momente später:

Bedienung:	Here is our menu, sir.
Gast:	Oh, that's not necessary.
Bedienung:	So I can already take your order?
Gast:	Yes, please. I would like to have something really German, you know. I'll have *"Eisbein with Sauerkraut"*, please.
Bedienung:	Very well, sir.

4

Bitte vervollständigen Sie diese Fragen.

Ein Gast betritt das Restaurant und möchte an seinem vorbestellten Tisch Platz nehmen. Die Bedienung fragt ihn in höflicher Weise nach seinem Namen.

What ______________________ your name, please?

Can you ______________________ me your name, please?

Would you ______________________ your name, please?

May I ______________________ your name, please?

Im weiteren Verlauf des Abends stellt die Bedienung noch weitere Fragen.

5

Formulieren Sie bitte mithilfe dieser Liste höfliche Fragen.

Can you tell me ... Can you give me ... Would you like to have ... Would you like to see ... Can I take ...	a an the your	aperitif coat dessert jacket menu order reservation number room number some more wine table wine list

426854

6

Geben Sie bitte die deutschen Sprechabsichten in diesen Dialogen auf Englisch wieder.

Bedienung	Gast
Grüßt (Zeit: 20:15 Uhr)	Good evening. I reserved a table for one.
Erfragt Namen	My name's Miller. Frank Miller!
Bittet um Garderobe / führt Gast zum Tisch	
Händigt Speisenkarte aus	Thanks!
Erkundigt sich nach der Bestellung	I'm afraid I can't read the German menu.
Fragt, ob er englische Speisenkarte wünscht	Oh yes, please, that would be really helpful.
Möchte Bestellung aufnehmen	Oh, yes. Certainly.

Bedienung	Gäste
Grüßt Gäste (20:15 Uhr): eine Frau und einen Mann	Mann: erwidert Gruß
Fragt, ob Reservierung vorliegt	Mann: verneint
Bietet Tisch vor dem Fenster an	Frau: akzeptiert
Bittet um Garderobe / führt Gäste zum Tisch	–
Bietet eine englische Speisenkarte an	Frau: kann Deutsch lesen
Erkundigt sich, ob ein Aperitif gewünscht wird	Frau: Campari Orange Mann: trockener Sherry
Serviert die Aperitifs	Mann: dankt
Möchte Bestellung aufnehmen	–

Dealing with Guests in the Restaurant: Paying

7

Bitte lesen Sie den nachstehenden Dialog.

Nach einem Essen wendet sich ein Gast aus einer Gruppe Geschäftsleute an die Bedienung.

Gast:	Miss, can I have the check please?
Bedienung:	Certainly, sir. How do you want to pay?
Gast:	In cash.
Bedienung:	And will you pay only for yourself?
Gast:	No, for the whole group please.
Bedienung:	Very well, sir.
	...
Bedienung:	Here is your check, sir.
Gast:	Oh dear, that's too much. I haven't got enough money on me. Can I pay by credit card?
Bedienung:	Certainly, sir.
Gast:	Good! Here is my card.
Bedienung:	Thank you, sir. I'll be back in a moment.

8

Vervollständigen Sie nun bitte die folgenden Fragen der Bedienung.

Ein Gast möchte zahlen ...	*... und die Bedienung fragt ihn nach der Zahlungsweise.*	
I want to pay now. Can I pay? Could I pay, please? I would like to pay! I'd like to pay! Can I have the bill? Could I have the bill, please?	• How would you ______________ to pay, ... • How do you ______________ to pay, ... • How ______________ you going to pay, ... • Do you ______________ to pay (in) cash or by credit card, ... • Would you like to pay ______________ ______________ , ...	madam/sir?

Ein Gast möchte wissen, ob er auf eine bestimmte Weise zahlen kann, ...
Can I pay cash? Can I pay by credit card? Do you accept traveler checks?

... und die Bedienung bestätigt ...	
No problem, That's alright, Certainly, Of course,	madam/sir.

... bzw. lehnt bedauernd ab.
I'm sorry, madam/sir, but • that's not possible. • we don't accept ...

426856

Dealing with Guests in the Restaurant: Paying

9

Geben Sie bitte die aufgeführten Sprechabsichten in diesem Dialog auf Englisch wieder.

Words and phrases you might find helpful:
change
included
receipt
service (charge)
VAT = value added tax

1. Gast	**2. Gast**	**Bedienung**
Möchte bezahlen		Will wissen, ob jeder einzeln bezahlt
	Jeder zahlt für sich selbst	Bittet um einen Moment Geduld
		Händigt die Rechnungen aus
	Möchte wissen, was die letzte Bemerkung auf der Rechnung bedeutet	Bedienung und Mehrwertsteuer im Preis eingeschlossen
	Fragt, ob er mit einer *Bust-Finance*-Kreditkarte bezahlen kann	Selbstverständlich
Bezahlt bar; Bedienung kann das Wechselgeld behalten		Bedankt sich
	Möchte eine Quittung	Entspricht dem Wunsch
Verabschiedet sich		
		Wünscht noch einen angenehmen Tag

10

Finden Sie bitte für die folgenden deutschen Begriffe jeweils die englischen Entsprechungen.

Kotelett	____________	of	____________	Rindfleisch
Schnitzel	____________		____________	Lamm(fleisch)
Filet	____________		____________	Hammelfleisch
Hachse/Haxe	____________		____________	Schweinefleisch
Keule	____________		____________	Kalbfleisch
Steak	____________			
Rücken	____________			

Schweineschnitzel ____________________

Kalbshachse ____________________

Lammkeule ____________________

Hammelkotelett ____________________

Rinderfilet ____________________

Schweinshaxe ____________________

Lammrücken ____________________

Schweinefilet ____________________

Kalbsfilet ____________________

Lammkotelett ____________________

Rinderkeule ____________________

Lammfilet ____________________

Hammelkeule ____________________

426858

11

Finden Sie bitte für die folgenden englischen bzw. deutschen Begriffe die Entsprechungen in der jeweils anderen Sprache.

___	calf's	brain	___
___	pig's	kidneys	___
		liver	___
		sweetbread	___
		tongue	___

Kalbszunge ___

Schweineleber ___

Kalbsbries ___

Schweinenieren ___

12

Übersetzen Sie bitte als vorbereitende Übung diese Gerichte mithilfe Ihrer Vokabellisten M1 – M16.

a) Kalbsbries mit Spinat und gefüllten Kartoffeln
b) Gekochter Spargel mit Schinken und Salzkartoffeln
c) Schweinebraten mit dicken Bohnen und Salzkartoffeln
d) Steak Tartar (rohes, durch den Wolf gedrehtes Rinderfilet)
e) (AE und BE!) Gegrilltes Hähnchen mit Pommes frites
f) Tafelspitz (gekochtes Rindfleisch)

Sie machen Ihre Ausbildung in einem Familienbetrieb, der eine etwas fantasielose Speisenkarte mit Gerichten der gutbürgerlichen Art bietet (→ M17). Sie bekommen den Auftrag, die Karte zu übersetzen.

13

Überlegen Sie bitte, ob Sie unter Umständen einiges erklären müssen (z. B. „Berliner Art", „Eisbein", „Rote Grütze" u. Ä.).

Words and phrases you might find helpful:

broiled	preservative
broth	sauce
coloring	sweetener
cream of ... soup	thickened
custard	

The Menu: Service

Ein Gast sitzt offensichtlich etwas hilflos vor einer Speisenkarte, die ein Betrieb der gehobenen Gastronomie seinen Gästen „zumutet" (→ M18 – M22), und bittet Sie ihm einiges zu erklären.

14

Versuchen Sie bitte sechs Gerichte dieser Karte einem Gast, der Deutsch nur teilweise lesen kann, zu ERKLÄREN – NICHT ZU ÜBERSETZEN.

Words and phrases you might find helpful:

bitter	selection
egg white	sweet
finger biscuits ['bɪskɪt]	well done
hot	well seasoned
light	whipped cream
medium	
rare	we serve ... with ...
raw	it is served on ...
salty	it's a combination of ... and ...

Überlegen Sie sich zunächst, welche Informationen der Gast wirklich benötigt, um sinnvoll eine Wahl treffen zu können. Unterstreichen Sie dann diese Stichwörter und übersetzen Sie sie ins Englische. Eventuell fehlendes Vokabular können Sie in einem Wörterbuch nachschlagen.

Formulieren Sie dann bitte englische Erklärungen mit Ihren eigenen Worten.

Zur Erinnerung: Bitte keine Übersetzung!

Als Anregung finden Sie hier das Beispiel „Gefüllte Tomaten".

Gefüllte Tomaten

*Wir servieren Ihnen zarteste Freiland<u>tomaten</u>
mit einer fein abgestimmten <u>Füllung</u> aus
köstlichen <u>Bananen</u>, fruchtiger <u>Ananas</u> und
einer Mischung erlesener <u>Nüsse</u>.
Abgerundet wird diese Komposition
von einer mit ein wenig <u>Zitrone aromatisierten
erfrischenden Creme</u>.*

€ 10,00

(fresh) tomatoes
stuffed with
bananas/pineapples
(mixed) nuts

fresh lemon cream

Gast: Excuse me, Miss, I understand *Tomaten, Bananen, Ananas* and all that, but I can't make anything of the rest. Could you please explain what all this means?

Bedienung: Well, sir, *Gefüllte Tomaten* are tomatoes stuffed with a mixture of, as you said, bananas, pineapples and nuts with a fresh lemon cream. It's very nice, indeed.

426860

Hier sind einige Phrasen, die im Umgang mit einem Gast hilfreich sein können.

Please, follow me to your table.
May I take your coat, miss?
May I take your orders now?
Have you got a reservation?
Here is our menu.
Good morning, sir.
Is everything alright?
Our menu.
This way, please.
Here you are.

Today I can recommend ...
Here you are.
Did you book a table?
Good afternoon, madam.
What would you like to drink?
Are you ready to order?
What would you like as an aperitif?
Can I help you with your jacket, madam?
The ... is very good/delicious/excellent.
Good evening, Mrs/Miss/Mr Fitzroy.

15 Ordnen Sie diese Phrasen nun bitte den unten aufgelisteten Sprechabsichten zu.

Welcoming guests ____________________
____
____

Asking them about a reservation ____________________
____

Offering to take jackets or coats ____________________
____

Leading them to their table ____________________
____

Asking them about an aperitif ____________________

Giving them the menu ____________________
____
____

Taking orders ____________________
____

Recommending dishes ____________________
____

Asking about drinks ____________________

Serving meals or drinks ____________________

Asking if everything is all right ____________________

16

Geben Sie bitte – mit Bezug auf die Speisenkarte M23 – die folgenden in Deutsch angegebenen Sprechabsichten inhaltlich vollständig auf Englisch wieder.

Words and phrases you might find helpful:

caramel	marinated/pickled
clear soup/consommé	ragout/stew
flambé/flambéed	sherbet/sorbet
gratinated/au gratin	snails

Dialogübung I *Zur Mittagszeit hat ein Gast an einem Tisch Platz genommen und liest in der Speisenkarte.*

Bedienung	**Gast**
„Guten Tag, mein Herr. Haben Sie schon gewählt?"	"Oh, 'Gutten Tak'. I'm sorry, but my German is not very good, so I don't understand your menu. Do you speak English?"
Sie wiederholen Begrüßung und Frage auf Englisch.	"Well, my problem is, I haven't got too much time. But I need something to eat. In fact, I'm terribly hungry."
Sie fragen, ob der Gast eine Vorspeise, einen Hauptgang und ein Dessert wünscht oder nur einen Hauptgang.	"I was thinking about a soup or a hot starter."
Sie empfehlen „Entenkraftbrühe mit Roter Bete".	"Oh no, that's absolutely horrible. I never eat poultry!"
Sie empfehlen eine andere Vorspeise.	"OK, that sounds good. I'll have that, please. And after that I need a solid main course. Could you please tell me what 'Geschnetzeltes Schweinefilet in Gorgonzolarahm mit Gemüsebukett und Kartoffelkroketten' is?"
Sie beantworten die Frage.	"Well, no. I don't think I would like this. Can you recommend anything else? But remember: no poultry, if you please!"
Sie empfehlen einen anderen Hauptgang.	"Yes, that's great; I'll take it, please. And that's all then."
Sie erwähnen, dass das Dessert mit den Kirschen köstlich ist.	"Hm ... well, I don't know. Oh all right, bring me that as well, please."
Sie fragen, welches Getränk der Gast wünscht.	"Just some mineral water, please."

426862

Dialogübung II *Ein Gast betritt um 18:30 Uhr das Restaurant.*

Bedienung	Gast
„Guten Abend, meine Dame/mein Herr. Kann ich Ihnen helfen?"	"Oh, hm ... well. I'm afraid I don't speak German too well. Do you speak English?"
Sie reagieren angemessen.	Sie möchten gerne zu Abend essen.
Sie fragen, ob eine Tischreservierung vorliegt.	Sie haben nicht reserviert.
Das Restaurant ist voll. Sie können dem Gast aber einen Platz an einem großen Tisch anbieten, an dem bereits drei Personen (Nichtraucher!) sitzen.	Sie sind Nichtraucher und akzeptieren das Angebot.
Sie führen den Gast zum Tisch.	–
Sie empfehlen als Vorspeise besonders „Honigmelone mit Schwarzwälder Rauchschinken".	Sie akzeptieren die Empfehlung.
	Sie wissen zwar, was „Lammkeule mit Kräutern" bedeutet, verstehen aber die restlichen Angaben zu diesem Gericht nicht.
Sie beantworten Fragen hinsichtlich der Karteneinträge.	Sie entscheiden sich dagegen und fragen, ob sie das Entrecote ... mit Kroketten statt mit Röstkartoffeln haben können.
Kleine Änderungen der Gerichte sind selbstverständlich möglich.	Sie bestellen dieses Gericht und möchten dazu ein Bier.
Sie fragen, ob der Gast ein Dessert wünscht.	Sie möchten zum Abschluss lediglich einen Kaffee, aber kein Dessert.
Zur Kontrolle wiederholen Sie die Bestellung des Gastes.	
Sie fragen, welches Bier der Gast wünscht.	Sie sind unsicher und möchten eine Empfehlung.
Sie empfehlen ein Pils.	Sie akzeptieren.

German Food

In einem Gespräch über Essensgewohnheiten, das Sie mit einem Gast führen, erkundigt er sich nach Gerichten, die „typisch deutsch" bzw. tyisch für „Ihre" Region sind.

17 Die folgenden Beispiele sollen Ihnen hierfür Anregungen geben.

Himmel un Ääd
(Himmel und Erde)

rheinisch

- Kartoffelbrei
- Apfelkompott
- gebratene Blutwurst
- gebratene Zwiebeln

- mashed potatoes
- apple sauce
- fried black pudding
- fried onions

Oh, that's quite a simple dish from the Rhine area, madam. It's mashed potatoes with apple sauce and fried black pudding and some fried onions. It's really lovely. (You see, the name means "heaven and earth"; the potatoes come from the soil and the apples from the opposite direction, the heaven.)

Labskaus

norddeutsch

- Pökelfleisch
- Kartoffelbrei
- Rote Bete

- corned meat
- mashed potatoes
- beetroot

That's a meal from northern Germany. It's a mixture of corned meat, mashed potatoes and beetroot. We serve it with a sour herring and a fried egg. I'm afraid not everyone likes it, but I love it.

Quarkkäulchen

sächsisch

- durchgepresste Kartoffeln
- Quark
- Eier
- Mehl
- Rosinen
- Vanillesoße
- Zucker und Zimt
- Vanilleeiscreme und Kirschen

- mashed potatoes
- curd
- eggs
- flour
- raisins
- custard
- sugar and cinnamon
- vanilla ice cream and cherries

They are a special kind of Saxonian dessert. You fry little cakes made mainly of mashed potatoes, curd, eggs, flour and raisins. We serve them with custard or with sugar and cinnamon or with vanilla ice-cream and cherries. Whatever you like better, sir.

426864

18

Versuchen Sie nun bitte die folgenden Gerichte in gleicher Weise wie oben zu beschreiben.

Words and phrases you might find helpful:

Austria/Austrian	rich
Baden/of Baden	specialty/(BE) speciality
bread cubes	Swabia/Swabian
broth	Switzerland/Swiss
pasta	

Maultaschen

schwäbisch/
badisch

- deutsche Art Teigwaren/Nudeln
- Rinderhack (manchmal mit Spinat gemischt)
- in Brühe

Kaiserschmarren

österreichisch

- süßer Pfannkuchen
- kleine Stücke
- sehr mächtig

Käsefondue

schweizerisch

- geschmolzener Schweizer Käse
- Schweizer Wein
- Knoblauch
- Cherry Brandy
- Brotwürfel
- lange Gabeln

Oder Dampfnudel, Leberknödel, Saumagen, Thüringer Klöße oder ... oder ... oder ...

Ein Gast möchte einen Wein bestellen. Da er mit der deutschsprachigen Weinkarte nichts anfangen kann, müssen Sie ihm die Weine kurz, aber präzise beschreiben.

19

Einige dieser Begriffe werden Sie sicherlich kennen. Die restlichen schlagen Sie bitte in einem Wörterbuch nach. Sie können diese Liste auch ergänzen.

rot rosé weiß	________ ________ ________
hell ↔ dunkel	________ ↔ ________
dünn ↔ ölig	________ ↔ ________
rau ↔ samtig	________ ↔ ________
stark ↔ schwach	________ ↔ ________
süß ↔ trocken	________ ↔ ________
fruchtig	________
Schaumwein	________
Jahrgang	________
________	________
________	________
________	________
________	________
________	________
________	________

Wine

20

Bitte übersetzen Sie zunächst die in der Tabelle angegebenen Stichwörter.

	Jahr	Farbe	Geruch	Geschmack
1	1982	Glänzend rot	Leicht nach Kirschen	Trocken/frisch/ sehr fruchtig
2	1987	Goldfarben	Fruchtig	Angenehm nach Äpfeln und Ananas
3	1984	Hell-goldfarben	Frisch	Trocken/frisch
4	1976	Tiefes Rot	Fein/fruchtig	Erdbeeren
5	1982	Helles Rot	Kirschen	Kirschen/Pflaumen

	Year	Color	Smell	Taste
1	1982 vintage	Brilliant red color	A little bit of cherries	Dry/fresh/very fruity
2				
3				
4				
5				

21

Beantworten Sie nun bitte die Fragen eines Gastes zu den Weinen auf der Karte Ihres Restaurants.

a) "What color is wine # 2?"
b) "How does wine # 3 taste?"
c) "Is wine # 3 very dry?"
d) "What kind of taste has wine # 4?"

22

Beschreiben Sie nun vier Weine – kurz und präzise – für eine englische Weinkarte Ihres Restaurants. Als Hilfestellung ist die Beschreibung von Wein Nr. 1 unten vorgegeben.

Gast: What can you tell me about wine # 1?
Bedienung: This 1982 vintage from Bordeaux has a brilliant red color and smells a little bit of cherries. The taste is dry and fresh but very fruity.

426868

Ein Gast ist über die Vielfalt deutscher Biere erstaunt und möchte sich bei Ihnen über die wichtigsten Merkmale deutscher Biersorten informieren.

23

Einige dieser Begriffe werden Sie sicherlich kennen. Die restlichen suchen Sie bitte aus einem Wörterbuch heraus. Falls Sie weitere Begriffe für wichtig halten, fügen Sie diese bitte Ihrer Liste hinzu.

hell ↔ dunkel	↔
stark ↔ schwach	↔
alkoholfrei	
Himbeersirup	
Hopfen	
Krone	
Malz	
obergäriges Bier	
untergäriges Bier	
Schaum	
Schuss	
Waldmeistersirup	
Weizen	

Beer

24

Bitte übersetzen Sie zunächst folgende Stichwörter und tragen Sie sie in die Tabelle ein.

Alt	Malzig, viel Hopfen, etwas bitter, dunkel, braun, obergärig
Berliner Weiße	Viel Schaum, mit einem Schuss Himbeer- oder Waldmeistersirup, fruchtig, sehr hell
Export	Hell wie Pils, untergärig, leicht herb, selten
Kölsch	Fein gehopft, aus Köln, sehr hell, goldfarben, obergärig
Pils	Klar, hell, goldgelb, untergärig, kräftig gehopft, hohe Krone
Weizenbier	Fruchtig, sehr hell, viel Schaum, obergärig, gutes Sommergetränk, evtl. mit einer Zitronenscheibe

	Aussehen	**Geschmack**	**Sonstiges**
Alt	Dark, brown	Malty, a lot of hops, a little bit bitter	Top-fermented
Berliner Weiße			
Export			
Kölsch			
Pils			
Weizenbier			

25

Beantworten Sie nun bitte die Fragen eines Gastes zu den einzelnen Bieren.

a) "What color is *Berliner Weiße*?"
b) "How does *Export* taste?"
c) "Has *Pils* a lot of froth?"
d) "What kind of taste has *Weizenbier*?"
e) "What does the name *Kölsch* mean?"

26

Beschreiben Sie nun – kurz und präzise – für Ihren Gast die Biere.

Gast: What's *Altbier*? You know, I want fresh beer and not old beer.
Bedienung: Oh no, sir, *Alt* is a dark brown, top-fermented beer. It is malty and has a lot of hops so that the taste is a little bit bitter.

426870

Bei der Arbeit in der Bar müssen Sie die verschiedensten Tätigkeiten mit unterschiedlichen Gerätschaften ausführen.

27

Finden Sie bitte die deutschen Ausdrücke für die hier genannten englischen Begriffe und Tätigkeiten.

	cocktail glass
	longdrink glass
	cocktail stick
	mixing glass
	bar spoon
	shaker
	mixer
	strainer
	crushed ice
	ice cubes
	measure
	• *dash*
	• *drop*
	• *one half*
	• *one quarter*
	• *three quarters*
	• *one fifth/two eighths, etc.*
	• *liter/centiliter/milliliter*
	• *teaspoon*
	• *tablespoon*
	to add
	to decorate
	to fill
	to mix
	to pour
	to shake
	to stir
	to strain

Cocktails

Ein schottischer Gast ist ganz begeistert von einem Cocktail, den Sie ihm serviert haben, und möchte nun wissen, was er alles enthält und wie er gemacht wird.

Bobby Burns

1/2 Scotch Whisky
1/2 Vermouth rosso
3 Tropfen Benedictine
Zitronen- bzw. Orangenschale

Die Zutaten werden in der oben genannten Reihenfolge in ein vorgekühltes Mixglas gegeben. Die Mixtur wird umgerührt und in ein Cocktailglas gegossen. Abschließend wird über dem Getränk die Zitronen- bzw. Orangenschale ausgedrückt.

"Well, sir, it's really easy. **First** take a cold mixing glass. **Then** fill in one half of Scotch Whisky **and then** one half of Vermouth rosso. **Next** add three drops of Benedictine. **After that** stir it well and pour it into a cocktail glass. And **finally** squeeze a lemon or orange peel over it. And that's all. Cheerio!"

28

Versuchen Sie nun bitte die Herstellung eines „Grand Slam" auf gleiche Weise zu beschreiben.

Grand Slam

1/2 Schwedenpunsch
1/4 Vermouth rosso
1/4 Vermouth dry

Die Zutaten werden in einem Shaker mit Würfeleis geschüttelt und dann in ein Cocktailglas abgeseiht.

First fill some ice cubes into a ______________________________ . **Next** add one half of

______________________________, **and then** ______________________ of Vermouth rosso

and ______________________________________ of Vermouth dry.

Then shake it and ________________________ it into a cocktail glass.

29

Suchen Sie sich bitte je einen gerührten, einen geschüttelten und einen gebauten Cocktail aus und geben Sie dann Anweisungen zu ihrer Herstellung.

426872

30

Ordnen Sie bitte die Nummern aus den Bildern M26/27 den jeweiligen Begriffen zu und finden Sie die deutschen Ausdrücke.

Breakfast products	Nr.	Frühstückswaren
bacon		
cereals		
• cornflakes		
• granola		
• oatmeal		
cheese		
coffee		
• decaffeinated		
cold cuts		
croissant		
egg		
• boiled		
• fried		
• poached		
• scrambled		
• sunny-side-up		
ham		
hash browns		
hot chocolate		
maple syrup		
milk		
• skim milk		
omelette		
orange juice		
pancake		
preserve		
• honey		
• jam		
• jelly		
• marmalade		
tea		
waffle		

Breakfast utensils	Nr.	Gerätschaften für das Frühstück
bread basket		
breakfast cup		
butter dish		
butter knife		
coffee pot		
egg-cup		
milk jug		
napkin		
preserve dish		
saucer		
side knife		
side plate		
spoon		
sugar bowl		
tea pot		
tea spoon		
toast rack		
tray		

Complaints and Special Wishes in the Restaurant

1. coffee	a) d) g)
2. egg	
3. salt on my table	
4. slice of bacon	
5. scrambled egg	
6. omelette	
7. corn flakes	
8. table	
9. orange juice	
10. tea	
11. fried egg	
12. breakfast	
13. hot chocolate	
14. milk	
15. cold cuts	
16. knife	
17. napkins	
18.	
19.	
20.	
21.	
22.	
23.	
24.	
25.	
26.	
27.	
28.	
29.	
30.	
31.	
32.	
33	
34.	
35.	

31

Welche Beschwerden können sich im Zusammenhang mit den links aufgelisteten Dingen ergeben? Bitte ordnen Sie die folgenden Beschwerden den einzelnen Gegenständen zu – wie bereits bei Nr. 1 vorgegeben. Falls Sie es für nötig halten, erweitern Sie ruhig die Liste.

a)	My ... isn't ready yet.
b)	My ... is not done.
c)	My ... is oversalted.
d)	My ... is lukewarm.
e)	The ... is spoilt.
f)	The ... is missing.
g)	The ... is tasteless.
h)	This ... is tough.
i)	This ... is burnt.
j)	My ... has not been cooked properly.
k)	I can't find any ... on the buffet.
l)	There is/are no ... on my table/the buffet.
m)	The ... has not been cleaned.
n)	
o)	

426874

Complaints and Special Wishes in the Restaurant

Ein Gast ruft einen Kellner und beschwert sich.

Gast:	Excuse me, sir, my coffee is only lukewarm.
Bedienung:	Oh, I'm very sorry to hear that. I'll bring you a new one in a second. I do apologize for that.

Beim Frühstück wendet sich ein Gast mit einer speziellen Bitte an eine Kellnerin.

Gast:	Excuse me, I'm a diabetic and I must not have any sugar in my coffee. Could you get me some sweetener?
Bedienung:	Certainly, miss, no problem. I'll bring you some immediately.
Gast:	That's very kind. Thank you very much indeed.
Bedienung:	You're welcome, miss.

32

Formulieren Sie jetzt bitte einige Beschwerden bzw. Extrawünsche sowie die angemessenen Reaktionen.

I'm	really very	sorry, sorry about that, sorry to hear that,	madam. miss. sir.

<table>
<tr><td colspan="3">I'll bring you</td><td>one
some
a new one</td><td rowspan="4">at once.
immediately.</td></tr>
<tr><td colspan="2">I'll</td><td>change
clean
fix</td><td rowspan="2">it
them</td></tr>
<tr><td>I'll ask</td><td>the chef
our head waiter
the manager</td><td>to fix
to make
to see to</td></tr>
<tr><td colspan="3">I'll see to it</td><td></td></tr>
<tr><td colspan="5">I'm afraid that's not possible, because ...</td></tr>
</table>

Describing the Hotel

Sie sind im **Frontoffice** *eingesetzt und müssen am Telefon Auskunft über „Ihr" Hotel geben.*

33 Beantworten Sie sich nun bitte gegenseitig folgende Fragen.

What type of hotel is it?	It's a	B & B business hotel conference hotel luxury hotel motel resort hotel spa hotel sports hotel	with	(160) rooms. (430) beds.

Where is the hotel?	It's	in the center on the outskirts	of the town/city. of (Düsseldorf).
		in the country, near the airport/station/...	

How can you get there?	It's (only)	ten minutes	by bus by car on foot	from the airport. ...

What are the surroundings like?	It's	very close to not far from next to near in	the a	center. quiet area. park. ...

What is the interior like?	Our hotel has We have	(160) rooms. (430) beds.	
	It's	very quite	elegant. modern. old fashioned. cozy.

426876

34

Versuchen Sie nun bitte „Ihr" Hotel **zusammenhängend** zu beschreiben. Sie können sich erst Notizen machen, die Sie anschließend in einen Text umsetzen.

Zunächst ein Beispiel:

Type of hotel:	business hotel
Rooms/beds:	220 rooms / 390 beds
Interior:	elegant but cozy / rooms with shower or bath, telephone, TV and minibar / restaurant with international cooking / indoor swimming pool / multigym
Where:	in the center / 5 minutes on foot from business center / 5 minutes on foot from shopping area

Gast: Can you give me some information about your hotel, miss?

Telefonistin: Well, madam. Our hotel is a business hotel with 220 elegant but very cozy rooms and a total of 390 beds. All our rooms have bath or shower, telephone, TV and a minibar. It's directly in the center of Düsseldorf, only 5 minutes on foot from the main shopping area and the business center. We have a restaurant with international cooking and an indoor swimming pool with a multigym.

Nun „Ihr" Hotel:

Type of hotel: ______________________

Rooms/beds: ______________________

Interior: ______________________

____

____

____

____

Where: ______________________

____

____

____

____

Giving Directions

Sie arbeiten an der Rezeption und müssen einem Gast, der soeben eingecheckt hat, die örtlichen Gegebenheiten erklären.

35

Finden Sie bitte auf der Grundlage des Hotelplans M30 für die fett gedruckten Ausdrücke in den folgenden Sätzen die jeweiligen deutschen Entsprechungen.

Words and phrases you might find helpful:

bar	reception
cloakroom	restaurant
conference room	stairs
elevator/(BE) lift	telephone
entrance	toilets
office	

The cloakroom is **on the left of** the restaurant. ____________________

On the right of the restaurant is the conference room. ____________________

Between the bar and the telephones are the toilets. ____________________

The reception and the offices are **in front of** the restaurant. ____________________

Behind the offices is the restaurant. ____________________

Opposite the bar is the cloakroom. ____________________

36

Vervollständigen Sie bitte die folgenden Sätze mithilfe des Hotelplans M30.

On the left of the restaurant is the ____________________

On the right of the elevators are the ____________________

Between the cloakroom and the conference room are the ____________________

The left entrance is between the ____________________

____

On the right of the bar you find the ____________________

Behind the reception are the

The restaurant is situated

The cloakroom is

The toilets are situated

You find the stairs

37

Nun beschreiben Sie bitte die Hotelhalle nach Plan M29.

Words and phrases you might find helpful:

behind the ...	in the back of the ...
between the ...	on the left (of the) ...
in front of the ...	on the right (of the) ...
in the ...	opposite the ...

38

Finden Sie bitte für die fett gedruckten Ausdrücke in den folgenden Sätzen die jeweiligen deutschen Entsprechungen.

Gäste wenden sich an Sie als Rezeptionist/-in, weil sie fremd in der Stadt sind und eine bestimmte Adresse suchen. Mithilfe eines Stadtplans (→ M32) geben Sie ihnen die nötigen Wegbeschreibungen.

Gast: Excuse me, could you tell me the way to the next bank?

Rezeptionist/-in: Well, certainly, sir. Leave the hotel by the main entrance, **turn left** and **go straight on.**

Then **turn right into** *Hauptstraße.*

Go **along** this street and you'll find the bank

on the left side.

Giving Directions

Gast:	Where do I find the cinema, please?	
Rezeptionist/-in:	That's in *Hauptstraße* **after** the department store.	______________
Gast:	And a place for my car?	
Rezeptionist/-in:	The car park is in the same street **behind** the theater.	______________
Gast:	You know, I like classical music very much.	
Rezeptionist/-in:	You're lucky, madam. Our opera is very good, indeed. It's in *Elisabethstraße*. Turn left when you leave the hotel and go along	______________
	Fürstenwall. **Cross** *Hauptstraße* and turn	______________
	right **at the next corner**. You'll see the opera	______________
	on the first corner on the left side.	______________

39

Zu welchen Zielen des Stadtplans M32 wollen die einzelnen Gäste?

	Wegbeschreibung	Ziel
1.	Leave the hotel and turn left into *Fürstenwall*, please. Then go straight on, cross *Hauptstraße* and turn left into the next street. Then it's on the right side after some hundred meters.	______________
2.	That's easy, madam. You know *Hauptstraße*, don't you. Turn right into *Hauptstraße*, keep going straight on, cross one street and it's the first big building on the right side.	______________
3.	Turn right when you leave the hotel. Go along *Fürstenwall.* Turn left into the second street, cross *Hauptstraße*, go straight on and you'll see it on your left, just before the corner of *Elisabethstraße*.	______________
4.	That's not far. Turn left into *Fürstenwall*, cross *Hauptstraße* and it's on your right, directly opposite the bus stop.	______________

426880

40

Formulieren Sie jetzt bitte selbstständig Wegbeschreibungen, zunächst noch nach dem Stadtplan M32. Wenn Sie sich sicherer fühlen, nehmen Sie bitte eine Karte Ihrer Stadt und erklären Sie die Wege von dem Hotel, in dem Sie Ihre Ausbildung machen, zu verschiedenen markanten Punkten der Stadt.

Die folgende Auflistung soll Ihnen einige Anregungen geben.

- Bahnhof
- Flughafen
- Einkaufszentren
- Geschäftszentren
  - Banken
  - Versicherungen
  - Fabriken
  - ...
- Restaurants
- Sehenswürdigkeiten
  - Nähere Ausflugsziele
  - Gebäude
  - Museen
  - Plätze
  - Parks
  - ...
- Sportstätten

Words and phrases you might find helpful:

go straight on	church
turn right/left (into ...)	• Anglican church
cross *Hauptstraße*	• Catholic church
go along *Fürstenwall*	• Protestant church
turn into *Friedrichstraße*	cinema
after the department store	exposition/fair ground
at the traffic light	factory
behind the theater	golf course
on the corner	level crossing
on the right/left (side)	main station
alley	opera
avenue	palace
brewery	pedestrians' area
car park	pedestrians' crossing
• multi storey car park	shopping mall
• underground car park	stadium
castle	subway/(BE) underground
cathedral	taxi stand
cemetery	tennis court
	theater/(BE) theatre
	theme park

Dealing with Guests in the Hotel

41

Bitte lesen Sie diesen Dialog.

Rezeptionist/-in:	Good afternoon, madam.
Gast:	Good afternoon. I booked a room.
Rezeptionist/-in:	Yes, what is your name, please.
Gast:	My name is Marilyn Monroe.
Rezeptionist/-in:	Oh, really?!?
Gast:	Really!!! That is my name.
Rezeptionist/-in:	Well, I see that room # 212 is reserved for you, madam. Could you please fill in the registration form?
Gast:	Yes, certainly.
Rezeptionist/-in:	Here is your keycard, madam.
Gast:	Thanks. Do you think I could have something to eat in my room?
Rezeptionist/-in:	Certainly, madam. Shall I call room service for you?
Gast:	That would be very nice. I only want some sandwiches, please.
Rezeptionist/-in:	No problem, madam.

Ein Gast checkt ein. An der Rezeption wird er **in höflicher Weise** *nach seinem Namen gefragt.*

42

Bitte vervollständigen Sie diese Fragen.

What ______________________________ your name, please?

Can you ______________________________ me your name, please?

Would you ______________________________ your name, please?

May I ______________________________ your name, please?

Bei Gesprächen an der Rezeption können sich verschiedene weitere Fragen ergeben.

43

Formulieren Sie bitte mithilfe dieser Liste höfliche Fragen.

Can you tell me ...? Can you give me ...? Would you like to have ...? Would you like to see ...? Can I take ...? Can I call ... for you? Shall I call ...?	address bus timetable city map credit card number hotel brochure passport number porter reservation number room number taxi tomorrow's program valuables to the safe

426882

44

Geben Sie bitte die deutschen Sprechabsichten in diesen Dialogen in Englisch wieder.

Rezeptionist/-in	Gast
Grüßt (Zeit: 16:23 Uhr)	Good afternoon. I booked a room.
Erfragt Namen	My name's Hardy. Oliver Hardy!
Bittet um Ausfüllen des Anmeldeformulars	Yes, certainly!
Händigt Schlüssel aus	Thank you very much.
Erkundigt sich nach besonderen Wünschen	None whatsoever, thank you.
Fragt, ob englischsprachige Stadtinformation gewünscht wird	Oh yes, please, that would be really helpful.

Rezeptionist/-in	Gast
Grüßt einen männlichen Gast (Zeit: 16:23 Uhr)	Erwidert Gruß, möchte ein Zimmer
Fragt, ob Reservierung vorliegt	Verneint
Bittet um Ausfüllen des Anmeldeformulars	–
Händigt Schlüssel für Zimmer 325 aus	Bedankt sich/fragt, ob das Zimmer ruhig ist
Bejaht/fragt, ob der Gepäckträger gerufen werden soll	Verneint/fragt, ob er Informationsmaterial über die Stadt haben kann
Stadtplan u. Ä. liegen auf dem Zimmer bereit	Bedankt sich

Dealing with Guests in the Hotel: Paying

45

Bitte lesen Sie den unten stehenden Dialog.

Gast:	Miss, I want to check out today. Can I have my check please?
Rezeptionist/-in:	Certainly, sir. How do you want to pay?
Gast:	Can I pay cash?
Rezeptionist/-in:	Certainly, sir, that's no problem.
Rezeptionist/-in:	Here is your check, sir.
Gast:	Oh dear, that's too much. I haven't got enough money on me. Can I pay by credit card? I have a *Bust Finance Card*?
Rezeptionist/-in:	Of course, sir, *Bust Finance* is fine.
Gast:	Good! Here is my card.
Rezeptionist/-in:	Thank you, sir. I'll be back in a moment.

46

Vervollständigen Sie nun bitte die folgenden Fragen der Rezeptionistin bzw. des Rezeptionisten.

Ein Gast möchte zahlen ...	*... und die Rezeptionistin/der Rezeptionist fragt nach der Zahlungsweise.*	
I want to pay now. Can I pay? Could I pay, please? I would like to pay! I'd like to pay! Can I have the bill? Could I have the bill, please?	• How would you ____________ to pay, ... • How do you ____________ to pay, ... • How ____________ you going to pay, ... • Do you ____________ to pay (in) cash or by credit card, ... • Would you like to pay ____________ ____________, ...	madam/sir?

426884

Ein Gast möchte wissen, ob er auf eine bestimmte Weise zahlen kann, …	*… und die Rezeptionistin/ der Rezeptionist bestätigt …*		*… bzw. lehnt bedauernd ab.*
Can I pay cash? Can I pay by credit card? Do you accept traveler's checks?	No problem, That's alright, Certainly, Of course,	madam/sir.	I'm sorry, madam/sir, but • that's not possible. • we don't accept …

47

Geben Sie bitte die aufgeführten Sprechabsichten im folgenden Dialog auf Englisch wieder.

Words and phrases you might find helpful:
Euro(s), € [jʊərəʊ/jʊərəʊz]
included
telephone call

Gast	Rezeptionist/-in
Möchte bezahlen	Fragt nach Zahlungsart
Bar	Selbstverständlich, bittet um einen Moment Geduld
	Kehrt zurück, händigt Rechnung aus
Fragt, ob auch die Telefongespräche auf der Rechnung stehen	Jawohl, zeigt sie dem Gast
Möchte doch mit Kreditkarte zahlen	Kein Problem
Händigt Karte aus	*Bust-Finance*-Card wird leider nicht angenommen
Ist ratlos, muss nun doch in Euro bezahlen	Ist selbstverständlich möglich

Complaints and Special Wishes in the Hotel

48

Ordnen Sie bitte die Nummern aus den Bildern M33/M34 den jeweiligen Begriffen zu und finden Sie die deutschen Ausdrücke.

Living Room/ Bedroom	Nr.	Wohn-/Schlafraum
air conditioning		
alarm clock		
ashtray		
bed table		
carpet		
coat hanger		
coffee table		
curtain		
cushion		
desk		
double bed		
dressing table		
fireplace		
heating		
lamp		
mattress		
minibar		
mirror		
pillow		
quilt		
radiator		
reading lamp		
rug		
sheet		
single bed		
sofa/settee		
telephone		
thermostat		
trouser press		
TV/television		
twin bed		
wardrobe		
wastepaper basket		

Bathroom	Nr.	Badezimmer
cistern		
comb		
faucet/(BE) tap		
flannel		
garbage bin		
mirror		
plug		
(electric) razor		
razorblade		
shampoo		
shower		
soap		
socket		
sponge		
toilet		
toilet roll/paper		
toilet seat		
toothbrush		
toothpaste		
towel		
washbasin		

49

Welche Beschwerdemöglichkeiten können sich im Zusammenhang mit den links aufgelisteten Gegenständen ergeben? Bitte ordnen Sie die folgenden Beschwerden den einzelnen Gegenständen zu – wie bereits bei Nr. 1 vorgegeben. Erweitern Sie ruhig die Liste.

1. air conditioning	a) d) g)
2. ashtray	
3. bed	
4. cistern	
5. heating	
6. lamp	
7. mirror	
8. reading lamp	
9. rug	
10. sheet	
11. toilet	
12. toilet roll	
13. toilet seat	
14. towel	
15. TV/television	
16. vase	
17. washbasin	
18. wastepaper basket	
19.	
20.	
21.	
22.	
23.	
24.	
25.	
26.	
27.	
28.	
29.	
30.	
31.	
32.	
33.	
34.	
35.	

a)	The ... doesn't work.
b)	The ... has not been made.
c)	The ... is empty.
d)	There is/are no ... in my room.
e)	The ... is full.
f)	The ... is broken.
g)	The ... is dirty.
h)	This ... is blocked.
i)	This ... is out of order.
j)	The ... has not been emptied.
k)	I can't find any ... in my room.
l)	The ... has not been cleaned.
m)	
n)	

Complaints and Special Wishes in the Hotel

Ein Gast ruft an der Rezeption mit einer Beschwerde an.

Gast: Excuse me, miss, but the bed in my room has not been made.
Rezeptionistin: Oh, I'm terribly sorry, madam. I'll send someone up to make it at once.

50 Formulieren Sie jetzt bitte einige Beschwerden und die angemessenen Reaktionen darauf.

I'm	very really	sorry, sorry about that, sorry to hear that,	madam. miss. sir.

I'll bring I'll send	one some	for you			at once. immediately.
I'll send	someone the chambermaid the ...	up to	change clean empty fix make	it them	
I'll ask	someone the chambermaid the ...	to			
I'll see to it					

Bei der Ankunft äußert ein Gast an der Rezeption eine spezielle Bitte.

Gast: I'm afraid I've forgotten to bring my soap! Could you get me some, please?
Rezeptionist/-in: Certainly, miss, no problem. I'll send some to your room.
Gast: That's very kind. Thank you very much indeed.
Rezeptionist/-in: You're welcome, miss

51 Formulieren Sie bitte zu den folgenden Stichwörtern Wünsche und reagieren Sie mithilfe der Liste in Übung Nr. 50 in angemessener Weise.

Words and phrases you might find helpful:

Wishes	Answers
• Can you get me ...? • Can you tell me ...? • I need ...	• I'll find ... • I'll get you ... • I'll send it ... • I'm afraid that's not possible ...

- A dirty blouse/shirt/skirt → Send it to a launderette
- Theater tickets for tomorrow night → Try to get some
- Flowers for a businessfriend's wife → Show way to flower shop
- An extra armchair for her/his room → Room too small
- A telephone/fax number → Look it up
- Departure time of plane/train → Give her/him a timetable

426888

Die Salesmanagerin, Meta Mustermann, hat Ihnen als ihrer Mitarbeiterin/ihrem Mitarbeiter einen Brief (→ M36) auf den Schreibtisch gelegt mit der Bitte, eine kurze deutschsprachige Notiz mit den wichtigsten Inhaltspunkten der Anfrage anzufertigen.

52

Füllen Sie bitte die einzelnen Punkte des folgenden Merkzettels aus. Unklare Begriffe schlagen Sie bitte in einem Wörterbuch nach.

NOTIZ

HAUS ZUR BRUCHBUDE

Datum ____________________

Brief/Fax/E-Mail/
Telefonat/Gespräch
von/mit ____________________

____

____

____

____

Anfrage/Reservierung/Beschwerde
Inhalt ____________________

____

____

____

____

____

____

____

____

____

Sonstiges ____________________

____

____

____

Der Sekretär Ole Olsen hat auf der Grundlage der nebenstehenden Notiz der Salesmanagerin als Antwort auf die Anfrage ein Angebot verfasst.

- *Bitte Schreiben der Leatherstocking Inc. beantworten*
- *Übliche Antwort mit Hotelprospekt und Preisliste*
- *Zusätzlich auf folgende Punkte hinweisen:*
  - *a) Preisnachlass von 15 % für Konferenzen mit mind. 50 Teilnehmern*
  - *b) Angebot: 3 Mahlzeiten pro Tag für € 155,00 pro Person*
  - *c) Möglichkeit zur Teilnahme am Musikfestival und Galadiner*

Mustermann

Als Mitarbeiter/-in der Salesmanagerin haben Sie die Aufgabe, alle Schreiben auf ihre Richtigkeit hin zu überprüfen, bevor sie ihr zur Unterschrift vorgelegt werden.

53 Markieren Sie bitte etwaige formale und inhaltliche Fehler.

Dear Mr Bumppo,

we thank you for your inquiry dated February 11 concerning a stay of 40 of your staff at our hotel.

For your information we are sending you our latest brochure as well as the current price list. Please, note that on conferences with not more than 50 members we can grant a reduction of 15 % on our standard price.
A special offer for your company are three meals at € 155.00 p.p./p.d. (all drinks included). As you are especially interested in leisure facilities we would like to point out that during the second week of your stay we would be happy to arrange for your group the booking of tickets for a concert of the "Festival of Classical Music" and a gala dinner. These open air concerts have a very good reputation and are regarded as among the best in the world; we enclose this year's programme and price list.

We hope that we could answer all your questions. In case any further ones should arise, please do not hesitate to contact us.

Sincerely yours,

Meta Mustermann
Sales Manager

54 Fertigen Sie bitte – ähnlich wie in Übung Nr. 52 – eine Notiz über den Inhalt der Anfrage M41 an.

426890

Zu Werbezwecken möchten die Restaurants der Stadt, in der Sie arbeiten, eine mehrsprachige Informationsbroschüre herausgeben. Sie werden gebeten für „Ihr" Restaurant einen englischen Beitrag vorzubereiten.

55

Entscheiden Sie zunächst bitte, welche Informationen für Ihren Beitrag wichtig sind. Streichen Sie in der nachfolgenden Liste Punkte, die nicht in Ihren Beitrag aufgenommen werden sollen, bzw. fügen Sie Ergänzungen hinzu.

Anzahl der Angestellten
Lage
Umgebung
Name des Küchenchefs
Restauranttyp
Name des Restaurants
Tätigkeitsbereiche der Angestellten
Einrichtung
Name des Besitzers
Anzahl der Plätze
Anfahrtsbeschreibung für Auto und/oder ÖPNV
Name des Geschäftsführers

____

____

____

____

____

56

Im Folgenden finden Sie Hilfen, die Ihnen die Beschreibung „Ihres" Restaurants erleichtern können. Ergänzen Sie gegebenenfalls diese Listen.

What type of restaurant is it?

- first class restaurant
- two star restaurant
- traditonal restaurant
- international restaurant
- local restaurant
- ______________________
- ______________________
- ______________________
- ______________________

Describing the Restaurant

Where is the restaurant?

- in the center
- on the outskirts
- in the country
- ______________________
- ______________________
- ______________________
- ______________________
- ______________________
- ______________________
- ______________________
- ______________________

How can you get there?

- on foot
- by bus/streetcar ...
- car
- car park
- How long does it take?
- ______________________
- ______________________
- ______________________
- ______________________
- ______________________
- ______________________

What are the surroundings like?

- busy streets
- quiet area
- park/shopping area/business center ...
- ______________________
- ______________________
- ______________________
- ______________________
- ______________________

426892

What is the interior like?

- elegant
- modern
- old fashioned
- cozy
- (fully) air conditioned
- number of seats
- ______________________
- ______________________
- ______________________
- ______________________

What is the food like?

- modern cooking
- international cooking
- regional cooking
- traditional cooking
- ______________________
- ______________________
- ______________________
- ______________________
- ______________________
- ______________________

Who works there?

- manager
- porters
- waiters
- receptionists
- chefs
- ______________________
- ______________________
- ______________________
- ______________________
- ______________________
- ______________________

Dealing with Guests in the Restaurant

57

Lesen Sie bitte diesen Dialog.

Dieser Dialog findet im Restaurant eines Hotels früh am Morgen statt. Mrs Gibson, ein Stammgast, kommt von ihrem Zimmer, um das Frühstück einzunehmen.

Bedienung:	Good morning, madam.
Gast:	Good morning.
Bedienung:	Did you sleep well?
Gast:	Well, actually I didn't. I couldn't get any sleep, because I had a terrible headache.
Bedienung:	I'm sorry to hear that.
Gast:	It's all my fault. I shouldn't have drunk so much of your marvellous *Altbier.* Well, maybe a good breakfast will make up for that. What've you got?
Bedienung:	Would you like to see our breakfast menu?
Gast:	No, thanks, I can't understand it anyway. Can you recommend anything light?
Bedienung:	Well, I could offer you some buttered toast. Or how about some eggs? We have scrambled, fried and boiled eggs.
Gast:	Oh, no eggs, please. First I'll have some cornflakes, with a lot of milk.
Bedienung:	Certainly, madam. And coffee, tea or cocoa?
Gast:	Coffee, please. A big mug of it.
Bedienung:	Very well, madam, I'll be back in an minute.

Einige Minuten später kehrt die Bedienung aus der Küche zurück:

Bedienung:	Here you are, madam.
Gast:	Oh thanks, that's exactly what I need right now.
Bedienung:	What would you like to follow?
Gast:	Maybe a few slices of toast with jam. And after that I'll see if my stomach can stand anything more.
Bedienung:	I'll see to it at once.

58

Schreiben Sie nun bitte die Wendungen heraus, die die Bedienung in den unten aufgelisteten Situationen benutzt.

a) Begrüßung
b) Höfliche Frage
c) Höfliche Aufforderung
d) Höfliche Empfehlung
e) Etwas aushändigen/etwas servieren

59

Jetzt überlegen Sie sich bitte noch weitere sinnvolle Wendungen und ergänzen Ihre Liste.

426894

Dealing with Guests in the Restaurant

60

Geben Sie bitte die Sprechabsichten von Gast und Bedienung auf Englisch wieder.

Zeit:	20:15 Uhr

Bedienung:	grüßt.
Gast:	• grüßt, • möchte Tisch für eine Person.
Bedienung:	fragt, ob reserviert wurde.
Gast:	bestätigt.

Bedienung:	• führt Gast zum Tisch, • händigt Speisenkarte aus.

Bedienung:	erkundigt sich nach der Bestellung.
Gast:	• kann deutsche Speisenkarte nicht so gut lesen, • erkundigt sich nach einem typisch deutschen Gericht.
Bedienung:	empfiehlt Rinderbraten (roast beef) mit gemischtem Gemüse und Kartoffeln.
Gast:	lehnt ab; möchte lieber ein Gericht mit Bohnen.
Bedienung:	bietet an, gleiches Gericht statt mit gemischtem Gemüse nur mit Bohnen zu servieren.
Gast:	• akzeptiert, • fragt, ob dazu ein Bier passt.
Bedienung:	• bestätigt, • fragt, ob „Pils" oder „Alt" bevorzugt wird.
Gast:	bestellt ein Pils.

Dealing with Guests in the Restaurant: Paying

61

Lesen Sie bitte zunächst wieder den Dialog.

Nach einem Essen wendet sich ein Gast aus einer Gruppe Geschäftsleute an die Bedienung.

Gast: Miss, can I have the check please?
Bedienung: Certainly, sir, do you want seperate checks?
Gast: No, I'd like to pay for all of us.
Bedienung: And how do you want to pay?
Gast: Oh, I think I'll pay cash.
Bedienung: Very well, sir.

Die Bedienung geht und kehrt nach einem kurzen Moment zurück:

Bedienung: Here is your check, sir.
Gast: Oh dear, that's more than I thought it would be. Unfortunately I haven't got enough cash on me. You wouldn't accept checks by any chance?
Bedienung: I'm afraid we can't do that, sir. But we accept all major credit cards.
Gast: I've only got a *Bust Finance* card.
Bedienung: That's absolutely no problem, sir, *Bust Finance* is perfectly alright.
Gast: Thank God for small mercies. By the way: tax is included?
Bedienung: Oh yes, VAT and service are included.
Gast: I see. Here you are then, my card.
Bedienung: Thank you, sir. I'll be back in a moment.

Nach einem kurzen Augenblick:

Bedienung: Here is your card, sir, and your receipt. Could you sign the receipt on this line here, please?
Gast: Of course. Here you are, then. Oh, and I have one last question.
Bedienung: Yes?
Gast: The first item on the check, what's that?
Bedienung: That's the cover charge, sir. It's a fee for the cutlery, the china, napkins and the like. We add it to each guest's check.
Gast: Oh, I see; I didn't know there was a thing like that. Well, I suppose we all of us have to make our living somehow. Here, this is for your remarkably friendly and attentive service.
Bedienung: Thank you very much indeed, sir. Have a nice day.

62

Schreiben Sie nun bitte die Wendungen heraus, die die Bedienung in den unten genannten Situationen benutzt, und ergänzen Sie anschließend Ihre Liste durch weitere sinnvolle Wendungen.

a) Frage nach getrennter oder gemeinsamer Rechnung
b) Präsentation der Rechnung
c) Frage nach der Zahlungsweise
d) Höfliche Ablehnung einer Zahlungsart
e) Akzeptieren einer Zahlungsart

426896

63

Erarbeiten Sie nun bitte einen Dialog, der die nachfolgend aufgelisteten Sprechabsichten ins Englische umsetzt.

Words and phrases you might find helpful:

bill, (BE) (bank) note	coin
by credit card	Euro(s), € [jʊərəʊ/jʊərəʊz]
(in) cash	item
change	

Eine Familie hat zu Mittag gegessen und möchte jetzt zahlen.

Gast: 1. bittet die Bedienung um die Rechnung.

Bedienung: 2. fragt nach der Zahlungsart.

Gast: 3. Kreditkarte; händigt Karte aus.

Bedienung: 4. bedauert, dass *Bust-Finance-Card* nicht akzeptiert werden kann.

Gast: 5. kein Problem, kann auch bar zahlen; händigt Geldnote aus.

Bedienung: 6. kann € 200,00 nicht wechseln, fragt ob evtl. kleinerer Schein vorhanden.

Gast: 7. leider nicht.

Bedienung: 8. bittet um einen Moment Geduld, muss ins Büro, um zu wechseln.

Gast: 9. soll sich ruhig Zeit lassen.

Bedienung: 10. kommt zurück; erklärt, dass sie leider mehr Münzgeld als normalerweise üblich zurückgeben muss.

Gast: 11. kein Problem; hat aber noch eine Frage.

Bedienung: 12. fragt höflich, worum es geht.

Gast: 13. hat den Eindruck, dass auf der Rechnung die zwei Portionen Eis für die Kinder vergessen wurden.

Bedienung: 14. vorletzter Punkt auf der Rechnung, „2 x Rumpelstilzchen-Becher", ist Kinderportion Eiscreme.

Gast: 15. ist beruhigt.

Bedienung: 16. will Wechselgeld aushändigen.

Gast: 17. nimmt nur die Scheine und bittet die Bedienung das Münzgeld zu behalten.

Bedienung: 18. weist darauf hin, dass es sehr viel ist.

Gast: 19. egal, bedankt sich für den hervorragenden Service.

Bedienung: 20. bedankt sich und wünscht einen guten Tag.

The Menu: Service

64

Übersetzen Sie bitte zunächst die folgenden Begriffe nach den vorgegebenen Mustern.

piece of meat	+	of	+	meat
escalope		*of*		*veal*

animal + 's	+	offal
pig's		*kidneys*

Lammkeule ______________________

Hammelkotelett ______________________

Schweinshaxe ______________________

Lammrücken ______________________

Schweinenieren ______________________

Kalbsfilet ______________________

Kalbszunge ______________________

Lammkotelett ______________________

Hammelkeule ______________________

Lammfilet ______________________

Schweineleber ______________________

Kalbsbries ______________________

Sie machen Ihre Ausbildung in einem Familienbetrieb, der eine etwas fantasielose Speisenkarte mit Gerichten der gutbürgerlichen Art bietet (→ M17). Sie bekommen den Auftrag, die Karte zu übersetzen.

65

Überlegen Sie bitte, ob Sie unter Umständen einiges erklären müssen (z. B. „Berliner Art", „Eisbein", „Rote Grütze" u. Ä.).

Words and phrases you might find helpful:	
broth	preservative
coloring	sweetener
cream of ... soup	to thicken
custard	

Ein Gast sitzt offensichtlich etwas hilflos vor einer Speisenkarte, die ein Betrieb der gehobenen Gastronomie seinen Gästen „zumutet" (➔ M18 – M22), und bittet Sie ihm einiges zu erklären.

66

Versuchen Sie bitte, sechs dieser Gerichte (sowie den Zusatz auf der Fischkarte) einem Gast, der Deutsch nur teilweise lesen kann, zu ERKLÄREN (KEINE ÜBERSETZUNG!). Überlegen Sie sich zunächst, welche Informationen der Gast wirklich benötigt, um sinnvoll eine Wahl treffen zu können, und formulieren Sie dann mit Ihren eigenen Worten auf Englisch. Als Anregung finden Sie hier das Beispiel „Gefüllte Tomaten".

Words and phrases you might find helpful:

bitter	selection
egg white	sweet
finger biscuits	well done
hot	well seasoned
light	whipped cream
medium	
rare	it is served on ...
raw	it's a combination of ... and ...
salty	we serve ... with ...

Gefüllte Tomaten

Wir servieren Ihnen zarteste Freilandtomaten mit einer fein abgestimmten Füllung aus köstlichen Bananen, fruchtiger Ananas und einer Mischung erlesener Nüsse. Abgerundet wird diese Komposition von einer mit ein wenig Zitrone aromatisierten erfrischenden Creme.

€ 10,00

(fresh) tomatoes
stuffed with
bananas/pineapples
(mixed) nuts

fresh lemon cream

Gast: Excuse me, miss, I understand *Tomaten, Bananen, Ananas* and all that, but I can't make anything of the rest. Could you please explain what all this means?

Bedienung: Well, sir, *Gefüllte Tomaten* are tomatoes stuffed with a mixture of, as you said, bananas, pineapples and nuts with a fresh lemon cream. It's very nice, indeed.

67

Geben Sie bitte – bezogen auf die Speisenkarte M23 – die folgenden deutschen Sprechabsichten inhaltlich vollständig auf Englisch wieder.

Words and phrases you might find helpful:

caramel	marinated/pickled
clear soup/consommé	ragout/stew
flambé/flambéed	sherbet/sorbet
gratinated/au gratin	snails

Dialogübung *Zur Mittagszeit hat ein Gast an einem Tisch Platz genommen und liest in der Speisenkarte.*

Bedienung	Gast
Sie grüßen auf Deutsch und fragen, ob die Dame bzw. der Herr schon gewählt hat.	Sie sprechen kaum Deutsch und benötigen Hilfe beim Lesen der Speisenkarte.
Sie wiederholen Begrüßung auf Englisch.	Sie haben zwar nicht viel Zeit, aber Sie sind sehr hungrig.
Sie fragen, ob der Gast eine Vorspeise, einen Hauptgang und ein Dessert wünscht oder nur einen Hauptgang.	Sie überlegen noch, ob Sie eine Suppe oder eine andere warme Vorspeise nehmen sollen.
Sie empfehlen „Entenkraftbrühe mit Roter Bete".	Sie mögen überhaupt kein Geflügel und lehnen entsetzt ab.
Sie empfehlen eine andere Vorspeise.	Sie akzeptieren den Vorschlag und fragen, was „Geschnetzeltes Schweinefilet in Gorgonzolarahm mit Gemüsebukett und Kartoffelkroketten" ist.
Sie beantworten die Frage.	Sie entscheiden sich dagegen und bitten um eine andere Empfehlung.
Sie empfehlen einen anderen Hauptgang.	Sie akzeptieren und sagen, dass das alles ist.
Sie erwähnen, dass das Dessert mit den Kirschen köstlich ist.	Sie sind zunächst etwas unschlüssig, nehmen dann aber doch dieses Dessert.
Sie fragen, welches Getränk der Gast wünscht.	Sie bestellen Mineralwasser.

68

Versuchen Sie nun bitte selbst Dialoge dieser Art zu erarbeiten.

4268100

69

Tragen Sie bitte die wichtigsten Fakten der Artikel in M 24 in die folgenden Tabellen ein.

	Meat/ Poultry	Fish	Corn/ Vegetables	Methods of Cooking	Others
North America					
Latin America					
Islamic Countries					
China					

International Food

	Meat/ Poultry	Fish	Corn/ Vegetables	Methods of Cooking	Others
Eastern Europe (in general)					
Czech Republic					
Hungary					
Poland					
Russia					
Slovakia					

4268102

	Meat/ Poultry	Fish	Corn/ Vegetables	Methods of Cooking	Others
Great Britain					
India & Southeast Asia & Pacific Region					
Ireland					
Israel					
Japan					

International Food

	Meat/ Poultry	Fish	Corn/ Vegetables	Methods of Cooking	Others
Mediterranean Countries					
Scandinavia (in general)					
Denmark					
Norway					
Sweden					

4268104

Sie geraten mit einem ausländischen Gast in ein Gespräch über die Küche seines Landes. Er zeigt ein sehr großes Interesse an diesem Thema und möchte nun seinerseits informiert werden über das, was typisch für die deutsche Küche ist.

70

Sammeln Sie nun bitte Fakten über die deutsche Küche im Allgemeinen bzw. die spezielle Küche Ihrer Heimatregion.

	Meat/ Poultry	Fish	Corn/ Vegetables	Methods of Cooking	Others
Germany (in general)					
Your Home Region					

71

Versuchen Sie nun bitte deutsches Essen (keine einzelnen Gerichte!) **mündlich** zu beschreiben.

International Food

Ein ausländischer Gast, der Deutsch nur unzureichend oder gar nicht spricht, sitzt in „Ihrem" Restaurant und möchte von Ihnen bei der Auswahl seines Essens beraten werden.

72

Wählen Sie zunächst eine Nationalität aus. Erkundigen Sie sich höflich und diskret, ob bzw. welche Ernährungsregeln der Gast befolgt, und beraten Sie ihn dann auf der Grundlage der Artikel über *International Food.*

Words and phrases you might find helpful:

basically	it is made from ...
mainly	it is made with ...
variety	it is served with ...
	you eat it with ...

Darüber hinaus erkundigt sich der Gast auch nach Gerichten, die „typisch deutsch" bzw. typisch für „Ihre" Region sind.

73

Die folgenden Beispiele sollen Ihnen hierfür Anregungen geben.

Himmel un Ääd (Himmel und Erde; rheinisch)
Oh, that's quite a simple dish from the Rhine area, madam. It's basically mashed potatoes with apple sauce, which sometimes is mixed with the mashed potatoes but here you get it as a side dish. With it we serve fried black pudding – which is made mainly from pig's blood – and some fried onions. It's really lovely. (You see, the name means "heaven and earth", and refers to the fact that the potatoes are taken from the soil and the apples from the opposite direction, the heaven).

Labskaus (norddeutsch)
That's a meal from northern Germany. It's a mixture of corned meat, mashed potatoes and beetroot, which you sometimes get as an extra on the side. We serve it with a sour herring and a fried egg. I'm afraid it's not up to everyone's taste, but personally I love it.

Quarkkäulchen (sächsisch)
They are a special kind of Saxonian dessert. You fry little cakes made mainly of mashed potatoes, curd, eggs, flour and raisins. We serve them either with custard or sugar and cinnamon or vanilla ice-cream and cherries. Whatever you may prefer, sir.

Käsefondue (schweizerisch)
Swiss specialty: melted Swiss cheese (Gruyère), Swiss wine, garlic and cherry brandy, bread-cubes, with special, long forks

Maultaschen (schwäbisch/badisch)
German kind of pasta, ground beef, in broth, sometimes meat with spinach

Kaiserschmarren (österreichisch)
sweet pancake, little pieces, very rich

Oder Dampfnudel oder Leberknödel oder Saumagen oder Thüringer Klöße oder ... oder ... oder ...

4268106

74

Bitte lesen Sie den nachfolgenden Text durch und tragen Sie die englischen Entsprechungen für die in der folgenden Liste vorgegebenen deutschen Ausdrücke ein.

Famous French wines are Champagne, claret and Burgundy. Champagne for example is a sparkling wine, whereas claret is a still red wine from the area of Bordeaux (the exact district has to be named on the label). Burgundy can be either a red wine or a white wine. Well-known German white wines are Rhine wine and Moselle (this word can stand for the wine as well as the river or the whole area). Quite popular all over the world are two fortified wines from Spain and Portugal, sherry and port.

There is no English word for a wine whose color is between red and white: it is called a rosé.

To keep the temperature of a sparkling wine or a white wine low you use a wine bucket or a champagne bucket.

aufgespriteter Wein	______________________________
(roter) Bordeauxwein	______________________________
Burgunder	______________________________
Champagner	______________________________
Etikett	______________________________
Moselwein	______________________________
Portwein	______________________________
Rheinwein	______________________________
Rosé	______________________________
Rotwein	______________________________
Sekt/Schaumwein	______________________________
Sektkühler	______________________________
Sherry	______________________________
Wein	______________________________
Weinkühler	______________________________
Weißwein	______________________________

75

Versuchen Sie bitte die Bedeutung des Wortes „*hock*" herauszufinden.

Für die englischsprachige Weinkarte „Ihres" Betriebes sollen Sie die dort aufgeführten Weine kurz beschreiben. Sie informieren sich in der einschlägigen Fachliteratur und finden die folgenden Charakterisierungen.

76

Tragen Sie bitte zunächst die wichtigsten Stichwörter zu den unten beschriebenen Weinen in die folgende Liste ein. Beschreiben Sie dann (wichtig: **nicht** übersetzen!) diese Weine in Englisch mit Ihren eigenen Worten.

Words and phrases you might find helpful:

acidity	finish	pineapple
balance	fresh	pleasant
balanced	fruity	ripe
brilliant	golden	ruby
claret	harmonic	tannic
colored, (BE) coloured	a hint of ...	a touch of ...
deep	-ish (e.g. greenish)	vintage
dry	nose	
to fade	on the palate	

1. Dieser rote Bordeaux des Jahrgangs 1982 weist eine glänzend rote Farbe auf. Er erinnert im Bukett ein bisschen an Kirschen, wobei er sich im Geschmack trocken und frisch, aber sehr fruchtig darstellt.
2. Die goldgelbe Farbe dieses Weins aus dem Jahr 1987 verliert ein bisschen durch einen leichten Stich ins Grünliche. Man wird jedoch entschädigt durch eine fruchtige Nase, sowie im Geschmack durch die angenehme Säure, die an Äpfel und Ananas erinnert.
3. Dieser goldfarbene 1984er ist im Bukett von einer säuerlichen Frische, die sich auf der Zunge bestätigt. Im Ganzen zeigt er sich jedoch überraschend harmonisch und ausgewogen.
4. Dieser 1985er besticht durch eine tiefrote Farbe, die ein bisschen zu Orange verblasst. Er weist eine feine, fruchtige Nase auf und erinnert im Geschmack deutlich an reife Erdbeeren.
5. Dieser rote Bordeaux aus dem Jahr 1982 präsentiert sich in einem funkelnden, tiefen Rubinrot. Das Bukett weist Anklänge an Kirschen und dunkle Beeren auf. Am Gaumen sind deutlich Tannine wahrnehmbar sowie Anklänge an Holz. Am eindrucksvollsten jedoch ist sein phänomenal langer Abgang.

	Year	Look	Smell	Taste	Others
1	1982	Brilliant red color	A touch of cherries	Dry, fresh, very fruity	Claret
2					
3					
4					
5					

4268108

77

Bitte lesen Sie den nachfolgenden Text durch und tragen Sie in der folgenden Liste die englischen Entsprechungen für die deutschen Ausdrücke ein.

The basic ingredient for making beer is malt: malt is made either of barley or – sometimes – of wheat or even of rye. The corn is soaked in water and heated up so that it starts to sprout (or germinate). To get malt this process has to be stopped again. This is done by kiln-drying.

The malt gets bruised (or rough-grinded). After that it is mixed with water and heated up. The mash, this is what this mixture of water and malt is called, has to be filtered to separate the wort from the sediment (the technical term is draff) which is often used as cattle-fodder.

The wort is mixed with hops and boiled, then cooled down again. The hops are necessary to provide the certain characteristic taste and to make sure that the beer has enough froth to make a good head on your beer. Yeast – either top-fermenting or bottom-fermenting yeast – is added to make the liquid ferment: and the result of all this is beer (depending on the yeast either top-fermented or bottom-fermented beer).

CHEERS!

darren	______________________
filtern	______________________
gären	______________________
Gärung	______________________
Gerste	______________________
Hefe	______________________
Hopfen	______________________
keimen	______________________
Krone	______________________
Malz	______________________
Maische	______________________
Roggen	______________________
Schaum	______________________
Treber	______________________
Weizen	______________________
Würze	______________________

Im Rahmen einer Spezialitätenwoche zum Thema „Bier" bietet „Ihr" Betrieb einige internationale Biere vom Fass. Sie bekommen den Auftrag, ein englisches Informationsblatt über deutsche Biere zu erstellen. In der einschlägigen Fachliteratur finden Sie folgende Informationen.

78 Suchen Sie bitte zunächst die wichtigsten Stichwörter zu den unten beschriebenen Bieren heraus und tragen Sie sie in die Liste auf Seite 111 ein.

Words and phrases you might find helpful:

alcohol • low alcohol contents • non-alcoholic beer • ordinary beer	dash finish flowery fruity	pale per cent raspberry strong
a lot of ...	hoppy	syrup
Bohemia	light	tart
bottom fermented	malty	top-fermented
cloves	maturation	woodruff
copper	not as much ... as	

Altbier heißt das kupferfarbene, herbe, obergärige Bier aus Norddeutschland – am besten schmeckt es in den gemütlichen Gastwirtschaften Düsseldorfs. Seine reinmalzige Milde und sein Hopfencharakter werden durch kühle Reifung schön abgerundet.

Kölns Bier – hell wie Pilsner, aber so fruchtig wie Ale – besitzt eine ihm ganz eigene, verlockende Delikatesse. Kann irgendein anderes Bier gleichzeitig als Aperitif und Digestif fungieren?

Ob es nun der Name erkennen lässt oder nicht, die meisten Biere der Welt sind helle Lagerbiere des Pilsner Typs, die das große böhmische Original mehr oder weniger getreulich nachahmen. Ein Pilsner ist jedoch mehr als nur ein helles Bier. Der echte Pilsner Stil zeigt Malzcharakter, ist aber in der Blumigkeit des Aromas und der Herbheit im Abgang hopfenbetont.

Berliner Weiße wirkt herrlich durstlöschend, etwa so wie frisch gepresster Zitronensaft am Mittelmeer oder Limonensaft in Florida. Für manchen Geschmack aber ist sie zu sauer und deshalb ist es Brauch geworden, einen Schuss Himbeersirup oder Waldmeisteraroma hineinzugeben.

Süddeutsches Weizenbier ist vor allem ein Sommergetränk. Es ist leicht und schäumend, hat die fruchtige Säure von Äpfeln und Pflaumen und erinnert oft an Gewürznelken. Klar oder naturtrüb, dunkel oder hell setzt es sich inzwischen überall in der Welt durch.

aus: Michael Jackson, Bier International, Hallwag, Bern/Stuttgart 1994

4268110

	Look	Taste	Others
Alt	Copper-coloured	Dry, mild malty, hop-character	Top-fermented, cold maturation, well balanced
Kölsch			
Pils			
Berliner Weiße			
Weizenbier			

79

Beschreiben Sie nun diese Biere in Englisch mit Ihren eigenen Worten (keine Übersetzung!).

Beer in English-speaking Countries

Here is some information about the most wide-spread types of beer made in English-speaking countries, which means not only in Great Britain but also in Ireland, North America, Australia, New Zealand and others.

Stout is a dry, strongly hopped beer with an almost creamy head. Its practically black color is achieved by adding not-malted, roasted barley to the mash. The brands best known in Germany are "Guinness" and "Murphy's".

A light version of Stout is **Porter**. It does not contain less alcohol, but its taste is not as strong as Stout's. The malt that is used for making Porter has been kiln-dried at a high temperature so that this beer is very dark.

In the United Kingdom the most popular beer is **Bitter**, which is a bit similar to our *Alt* in color and taste. In general, you can find Bitters of almost any character; what they all have in common is that they are strongly hopped.

Lager is a pale type of beer with not too much hops so that it has a very mild taste. It was originally brewed in Germany and can best be compared to *Pils*.

Ale is a light-colored beer, which is usually stronger in its content of alcohol and its taste than other beers.

Cocktails

Bei der Arbeit in der Bar müssen Sie die verschiedensten Tätigkeiten mit unterschiedlichen Gerätschaften ausführen.

80 Finden Sie bitte die deutschen Entsprechungen für die hier genannten englischen Begriffe und Tätigkeiten. Falls nötig ergänzen Sie die Liste.

____________	*cocktail stick*
____________	*mixing glass*
____________	*bar spoon*
____________	*shaker*
____________	*strainer*
____________	*crushed ice*
____________	*ice cubes*
____________	*measure*
____________	• *dash*
____________	• *drop*
____________	• *one half*
____________	• *one quarter*
____________	• *three quarters*
____________	• *one fifth/two eighths etc.*
____________	• *liter/centiliter/milliliter*
____________	• *teaspoon*
____________	• *tablespoon*
____________	*to add*
____________	*to pour*
____________	*to shake*
____________	*to stir*
____________	*to strain*
____________	____________
____________	____________
____________	____________
____________	____________
____________	____________
____________	____________

Ein schottischer Gast ist ganz begeistert von einem Cocktail, den Sie ihm serviert haben, und möchte nun wissen, was er alles enthält und wie er gemacht wird.

Bobby Burns

1/2 Scotch Whisky
1/2 Vermouth rosso
3 Tropfen Benedictine
Zitronen- bzw. Orangenschale

Die Zutaten werden in der oben genannten Reihenfolge in ein vorgekühltes Mixglas gegeben. Die Mixtur wird umgerührt und in ein Cocktailglas gegossen. Abschließend wird über dem Getränk die Zitronen- bzw. Orangenschale ausgedrückt.

81

Beschreiben Sie nun bitte die Herstellung des Cocktails.

„Well, sir, it's really easy. **First** take a cold ____________________. **Then** fill in one half of ____________________ **and then** ____________________ of Vermouth rosso. **Next** add ____________________ of Benedictine. **After that** ____________________ it well and pour it into a ____________________. And **finally** squeeze a lemon or orange peel over it. And that's all. Cheerio!"

82

Beschreiben Sie nun bitte den folgenden Cocktail ebenso.

Words and Phrases you might find helpfull:
first/second/third ...
then
after that
next
finally

Grand Slam

1/2 Schwedenpunsch
1/4 Vermouth rosso
1/4 Vermouth dry

Die Zutaten werden in einem Shaker mit Eiswürfeln geschüttelt und dann in ein Cocktailglas abgeseiht.

83

Ordnen Sie bitte die Nummern aus den Bildern M26/M27 den jeweiligen Begriffen zu und finden Sie die deutschen Ausdrücke.

Breakfast products	Nr.	Frühstückswaren
bacon		
cereal		
• cornflakes		
• granola		
• oatmeal		
cheese		
coffee		
• decaffeinated		
cold cuts		
croissant		
egg		
• boiled		
• fried		
• poached		
• scrambled		
• sunny-side-up		
ham		
hash browns		
hot chocolate		
maple syrup		
milk		
• skim milk		
omelette		
orange juice		
pancake		
preserve		
• honey		
• jam		
• jelly		
• marmalade		
tea		
waffle		

Breakfast utensils	Nr.	Gerätschaften für das Frühstück
bread basket		
breakfast cup		
butter dish		
butter knife		
coffee pot		
egg-cup		
milk jug		
napkin		
preserve dish		
saucer		
side knife		
side plate		
spoon		
sugar bowl		
tea pot		
tea spoon		
toast rack		
tray		

Complaints and Special Wishes in the Restaurant

84

Unten sind Möglichkeiten für Beschwerdegründe und Sonderwünsche vorgegeben. Welche weiteren Beispiele können sich im Zusammenhang mit dem Frühstück ergeben?

Words and phrases you might find helpful:

burnt	oversalted	... has not been cleaned.
lukewarm	tasteless	There is no ... on my table.
missing	tough	I can't find any ... on the buffet.
not done	spoilt	... has not been cooked properly.
not ready yet		

Complaints and Special Wishes in the Restaurant

85

Spielen Sie jetzt bitte in kurzen Dialogen einige Beschwerden bzw. Sonderwünsche sowie die entsprechenden Reaktionen durch. Unten sind Möglichkeiten für Reaktionen der Bedienung vorgegeben und außerdem als Anregung je ein Beispiel für eine Beschwerde sowie einen Sonderwunsch.

Words and phrases you might find helpful:

... really sorry about that ...	... clean it ...
... very sorry to hear that ...	... get you ...
... ask the chef to ...	... see to it ...
... bring you ...	... not possible, because ...
... change it ...	

Ein Gast ruft einen Kellner und bringt eine Beschwerde vor.

Gast: Excuse me, sir, my coffee is only lukewarm.

Bedienung: Oh I'm very sorry. **I'll** bring you a new one in a second.
I do apologize for that.

Beim Frühstück wendet sich ein Gast mit einer speziellen Bitte an eine Kellnerin.

Gast: Excuse me, I'm a diabetic and I'm not supposed to have any sugar in my coffee. Could you get me some sweetener?

Bedienung: **Certainly,** miss, **no problem**. I'll bring you some immediately.

Gast: That's very kind. Thank you very much indeed.

Bedienung: You're welcome, miss.

4268116

„Ihr" Hotel möchte sich mit einer Seite im Internet präsentieren. Das Salesoffice bekommt von der Hotelleitung den Auftrag, einen Textentwurf für den Interneteintrag vorzubereiten. Als Mitarbeiter in diesem Team sind Sie dafür zuständig, einen solchen Entwurf auf Englisch zu präsentieren.

86

Lesen Sie bitte zunächst die Zitate aus einer Broschüre des *Alto Motel* in *Gatlinburg, Tennessee* (→ M28).

87

Streichen Sie aus der folgenden Auflistung die Stichpunkte, die Ihnen unwichtig erscheinen, und ergänzen Sie gegebenenfalls Fehlendes. Tragen Sie dann die Stichwörter in die Liste auf der rechten Seite in der Reihenfolge ein, in der sie in Ihrer Broschüre erscheinen sollen.

leisure facilities	______
address	______
type of hotel	______
conference facilities	______
banqueting facilities	______
prices	______
number of staff	______
location	______
surroundings	______
special services	______
restaurant (type, size ...)	______
name of general manager	______
accessibility (by car, train, plane ...)	______
building (size, style, period ...)	______
______	______
______	______
______	______
______	______
______	______

Describing the Hotel

88

Tragen Sie bitte die jeweilige deutsche Übersetzung für die einzelnen Hotelbezeichnungen sowie die Nummern der entsprechenden Definitionen in die Tabelle ein.

Deutsche Hotelbezeichnung	Englische Hotelbezeichnung	Definition Nr.
	B & B	
	business hotel	
	boarding house	
	conference hotel	
	country house hotel	
	guest house	
	hostel	
	inn	
	luxury hotel	
	motel	
	resort hotel	
	spa hotel	
	sports hotel	

1. A hotel that provides as a special service treatments for ailments and diseases
2. A hotel which caters for the special needs of businessmen and -women
3. A hotel with furnishing, equipment and service of the highest level
4. A hotel on a somewhat smaller scale – mostly privately owned – which very often provides a personal and informal atmosphere
5. A kind of hotel which has been installed in a luxurious house in the country and which offers accommodation on a higher level
6. A hotel that offers parking place very often directly in front of the guest's room; in countries where people drive long distances
7. A hotel which offers facilities designed especially to answer to the needs of tourists
8. A hotel that has all the necessary facilities for any kind of meeting (business or otherwise)
9. A pub – usually in the countryside – that offers a few rooms as accommodation
10. A hotel with all the necessary facilities for certain kinds of sport
11. A hotel or guest house – sometimes even only one or two rooms in a private house – where the only meal on offer is breakfast;
12. A kind of hotel which offers accommodation for a longer period of time so people can live there and do not stay only a few nights
13. A "hotel" that offers cheap accommodation and meals, very often for special groups of guests: youth ~, students' ~ etc.

4268118

89

Im Folgenden finden sie Hilfen, die Ihnen die Beschreibung „Ihres" Hotels erleichtern können. Ergänzen Sie gegebenenfalls diese Liste.

What type of hotel is it?

- resort hotel/business hotel ...

Where is the hotel?

- in the center/on the outskirts
- in the country
- near a .../close to the ...
- ______________________________
- ______________________________
- ______________________________
- ______________________________
- ______________________________

How can you get there?

- on foot
- by bus/streetcar/car
- car park
- How long does it take?
- ______________________________
- ______________________________
- ______________________________
- ______________________________

What are the surroundings like?

- busy streets/quiet area
- park/cathedral/shopping area
- ______________________________
- ______________________________
- ______________________________
- ______________________________

Describing the Hotel

What is the interior like?

- How many rooms/beds?
- elegant/comfortable
- modern/old fashioned
- ______________________________
- ______________________________
- ______________________________
- ______________________________
- ______________________________

What is the restaurant like?

- How many seats?
- modern/old fashioned
- cozy
- the kind of cooking (modern, traditional, regional, international)
- ______________________________
- ______________________________
- ______________________________
- ______________________________
- ______________________________

Who works there?

- manager
- receptionists/porters
- chambermaids
- waiters/chefs
- ______________________________
- ______________________________
- ______________________________
- ______________________________

Als Anregung für „Ihren" Eintrag im Internet kann Ihnen der Text über das Lancaster Hotel in Houston, Texas (→ M28) dienen.

4268120

Ein Gast hat soeben eingecheckt. Er stellt nun Fragen über das Hotel. Da Sie im Moment keine englischen Broschüren zur Hand haben, müssen Sie ihm die örtlichen Gegebenheiten erklären.

Gast:	Where do I find the telephones, please?
Rezeptionist/-in:	There's one in your room of course and here in the lobby they're over there, sir, right opposite the reception.
Gast:	Oh, I see. And the conference room?
Rezeptionist/-in:	That's here on the left, just around the corner.

90

Formulieren Sie nun in der oben vorgegebenen Art Fragen und Antworten auf der Grundlage des Hotelplans M30.

Words and phrases you might find helpful:

at the back	on the left/right (side) of ...	You find the ...
between	opposite	
next to		

91

Überlegen Sie nun bitte, welche *hotel facilities* in einem Hotel – z. B. in „Ihrem" Betrieb – zu finden sind, und tragen Sie sie sowohl in Deutsch als auch in Englisch in die Liste ein.

Hotel facilities	Hoteleinrichtungen
florist's	
multigym	
newsstand	

Giving Directions

92

Setzen Sie nun Übung Nr. 90 mit dem Hotelplan M31 fort und beantworten Sie auch die unten aufgeführten weiteren Fragen mithilfe der angegebenen Stichwörter.

Words and phrases you might find helpful:

go straight on/along	center/(BE) centre
take bus number ...	high level
turn left/right	on foot
	opening hours
usual	park grounds
bus stop	regional meals
by bus	streetcar/(BE) tram

"Where is the the breakfast room, please?"	→	Im „Restaurant an der Ecke"
"And at what time do you serve breakfast?"	→	07:30 – 10:30; Buffet: € 15,50
"How can I get from here to the fair ground?"	→	Bushaltestelle vom Ausgang nach rechts, 5 Minuten zu Fuß; 12 Minuten Fahrt zur Messe mit Bus Nr. 68
"And to the city center?"	→	17 Minuten zum Stadtzentrum; Straßenbahn Nr. 34
"I see that you've got two restaurants. What's the difference between them?"	→	„Restaurant an der Ecke": regional typische Gerichte; „Gartenrestaurant": internationale Küche auf hohem Niveau
"How can I call room service?"	→	Telefonnummer 123
"Is there a book shop around here?"	→	In der Ladenpassage; normale Öffnungszeiten
"Can you tell me something about the surroundings?"	→	Großzügiger Park hinter dem Hotel
"But first of all I'd like to have a drink!"	→	Bar gleich gegenüber der Rezeption

4268122

93

Formulieren Sie nun in der unten vorgegebenen Art Fragen und Antworten auf der Grundlage des Stadtplans M32. Nehmen Sie anschließend bitte eine Karte „Ihrer" Stadt und erklären Sie die Wege von dem Hotel, in dem Sie Ihre Ausbildung machen, zu verschiedenen markanten Punkten der Stadt. Die folgende Auflistung soll Ihnen einige Anregungen geben.

• Bahnhof • Flughafen • Geschäftszentren (Banken, Versicherungen, Fabriken ...) • Einkaufsmöglichkeiten • Restaurants • Sehenswürdigkeiten (nähere Ausflugsziele, Gebäude, Museen, Plätze, Parks ...) • Sportstätten

Words and phrases you might find helpful:

go straight on	alley	golf course
turn right/left (into ...)	avenue	level crossing
	brewery	main station
cross *Hauptstraße*	car park	opera
go along *Fürstenwall*	• multi storey car park	palace
turn into *Friedrichstraße*	• underground car park	pedestrians' area
	castle	pedestrians' crossing
after the department store	cathedral	shopping mall
at the traffic light	cemetery	stadium
behind the theater	church	subway/(BE) underground
on the corner	• Anglican church	
on the right/left (side)	• Catholic church	taxi stand
	• Protestant church	tennis court
	cinema	theater/(BE) theatre
	exposition/fair ground	theme park

Ein Gast wendet sich an Sie als Rezeptionist/-in, weil er fremd in der Stadt ist und eine bestimmte Adresse sucht.

Gast: Excuse me, could you tell me the way to the exposition ground?

Rezeptionist/-in: Well, certainly, sir. If you leave the Hotel by the main entrance, you turn left. After some 100 meters there will be a traffic light. You cross *Hauptstraße* and walk to the bus stop.

Gast: Which bus do I take?

Rezeptionist/-in: You take # 708, which will take you straight to the exposition ground.

Gast: Well, I'm almost sure to find it with an explanation like this. But I have one more question: I've been told that there is quite an interesting museum around here.

Rezeptionist/-in: Yes, that's true; it's right opposite the bus stop.

Gast: Thank you very much.

Rezeptionist/-in: You're welcome, sir. Have a nice day.

Dealing with Guests in the Hotel

Dieser Dialog findet in einem Hotel um 16:00 Uhr statt. Sie stehen an der Rezeption und Mrs Gibson, ein Stammgast, betritt die Hotelhalle.

94

Lesen Sie bitte diesen Dialog.

Rezeptionist/-in:	Good afternoon, Mrs Gibson.
Gast:	Hi, here I am again. How're you doing?
Rezeptionist/-in:	I'm fine. How about you? It's nice to see you again. It's been quite a long time.
Gast:	Well, that's true. It's been almost eight months.
Rezeptionist/-in:	You've got a reservation, haven't you?
Gast:	Yes, I have. Can I have my regular room?
Rezeptionist/-in:	I'm afraid not, but you can have a room right next to it.
Gast:	Oh, that's all right. It doesn't have to be the same one, as long as it's away from the street.
Rezeptionist/-in:	Yes, of course it is. Could you please fill in the reservation form.
Gast:	Sure. This room has the same price, hasn't it?
Rezeptionist/-in:	It certainly has: € 370.00 for you.
Gast:	That's good; at least this hasn't changed. You're still the most expensive place in town.
Rezeptionist/-in:	According to your reservation you're going to stay for fourteen days.
Gast:	For a fortnight, yes. But I might be leaving a little bit earlier this time.
Rezeptionist/-in:	That'll be no problem, madam.
Gast:	Good. This time I've got a lot of baggage.
Rezeptionist/-in:	Would you like me to call the porter? He'll take care of it.
Gast:	That's great, so I won't have to wait here and can go right up to my room.
Rezeptionist/-in:	Shall I call someone to show you your room?
Gast:	Don't worry. I've been here quite a few times before, remember. I don't suppose you've changed the elevator to the other side.
Rezeptionist/-in:	Here's your key, madam. Have a nice stay.
Gast:	Thanks a lot. See you later.

95

Schreiben Sie nun bitte die Wendungen heraus, die die/der Hotelangestellte in den unten aufgelisteten Situationen benutzt.

a) Begrüßung
b) Höfliche Frage
c) Höfliche Aufforderung
d) Höfliche Empfehlung
e) Etwas aushändigen

96

Jetzt überlegen Sie sich bitte noch weitere sinnvolle Wendungen und ergänzen Ihre Liste.

97

Entwickeln Sie nun bitte einen alternativen Dialog zu dem auf der vorigen Seite, indem Sie die unten angegebenen Sprechabsichten, soweit es Ihnen möglich ist, in anderer Weise als in Nr. 94 auf Englisch umsetzen.

Zeit:	*16:00 Uhr*

Rezeptionist/-in:	grüßt.
Gast:	• grüßt, • fragt, wie es geht.
Rezeptionist/-in:	• antwortet, • erkundigt sich ebenfalls nach dem Befinden.

Rezeptionist/-in:	fragt, ob Reservierung vorliegt.
Gast:	• bestätigt, • fragt, ob der übliche Raum frei ist.
Rezeptionist/-in:	• bedauert, dass nicht, • Nachbarraum ist frei.
Gast:	akzeptiert, falls gleicher Preis.
Rezeptionist/-in:	selbstverständlich.

Rezeptionist/-in:	fragt, ob wieder 14 Tage Aufenthalt.
Gast:	• bestätigt, • eventuell etwas frühere Abreise.
Rezeptionist/-in:	kein Problem.
Gast:	hat diesmal viel Gepäck; bittet um Hilfe.
Rezeptionist/-in:	• ruft Pagen, • überreicht Schlüssel, • wünscht angenehmen Aufenthalt.

Dealing with Guests in the Hotel: Paying

Mrs Gibson, der Stammgast mit den höchsten Trinkgeldern, kommt vor dem Frühstück an die Rezeption.

98 Lesen Sie bitte zunächst wieder den Dialog.

Gast: Excuse me, you know that I want to leave today. Did you prepare my check?

Rezeptionst/-in: Yes, madam, we did. Here it is. Everything's ready for your check-out. I take it you want to pay by credit card as usual?

Gast: Exactly. Now let me see: yes, that's right, I had three of those tiny little gin bottles from the minibar and five Bitter Lemons. It's astonishing what you charge for them. Are you sure that's legal?

Rezeptionst/-in: Frankly, madam, and just between the two of us: it's not, but this way I can make a bit of money on the side.

Gast: Oh right; good, I'm always glad to see some initiative in young people. Well, where is my credit card? Oh my, I seem to have left it in my room. I'll just pop up and get it. I won't be a minute.

Rezeptionst/-in: That's alright, Mrs Gibson.

Nach einigen Minuten:

Gast: Oh my, that's most embarrassing. I can't find my credit card. I'm sure I lost it somewhere. Oh dear, oh dear.

Rezeptionst/-in: I'm sorry to hear that. Do you want me to call the credit card company and make sure they freeze your card?

Gast: Yes, please, that'd be very kind. But this doesn't solve the problem of my check. I have to pay you somehow and I have only this *Bust Finance Card.*

Rezeptionst/-in: I'm afraid we can't accept those. You don't happen to have any traveler's checks?

Gast: No, I don't. And I haven't got enough cash. Oh my, that's too unfortunate.

Rezeptionst/-in: I don't think that's a problem, madam. Being a regular guest of our house you can check out now and pay by bank transfer as soon as you're home.

Gast: Do you think so?

Rezeptionst/-in: Why! Certainly, Mrs Gibson. That's no problem at all.

Gast: Oh, you're taking some weight off my mind. Thank you very much indeed!

Rezeptionst/-in: That's perfectly alright, Mrs Gibson. Please don't mention it. I'm glad I could ease your mind on that point. And now I'll call your credit card company to see to the freezing of your card.

Gast: Oh yes, please, you're really very kind.

Rezeptionst/-in: Not at all, madam.

Nach dem Frühstück:

Gast: Listen, I'm sure I don't want to make a nuisance of myself, but I have one question concerning my check.

Rezeptionst/-in: Yes Mrs Gibson, what is it?

Gast: Here, this item. What's that? Mind you, I'm not complaining or anything like that; it's just that my German is so very poor and I don't understand what this word here means.

Rezeptionst/-in: Ah yes, you remember that you asked us to take your coat to the cleaners. The expression *Chemische Reinigung* means "dry-cleaning".

Gast: Oh yes, I see. Thanks for telling me.

Rezeptionst/-in: No problem, madam. You know we always endeavor to give satisfaction.

Gast: Gee! That sounds great. Hearing you talk like that, I'm sure you're destined for something big.

Rezeptionst/-in: Well, I got that phrase from a book. But who knows, maybe you're right and one of these days I'll be an assistant to the second deputy head receptionist.

4268126

99

Schreiben Sie nun bitte die Wendungen heraus, die die/der Hotelangestellte in den unten aufgelisteten Situationen benutzt.

a) Präsentation der Rechnung
b) Frage nach der Zahlungsweise
c) Höfliche Ablehnung einer Zahlungsart
d) Akzeptieren einer Zahlungsart

100

Jetzt überlegen Sie sich bitte noch weitere sinnvolle Wendungen für diese sowie gegebenenfalls andere Situationen und ergänzen Ihre Liste.

101

Erarbeiten Sie nun bitte einen Dialog, der die folgenden Sprechabsichten ins Englische umsetzt.

Ein Gast, der zum ersten Mal in „Ihrem" Hotel gewohnt hat, kommt an die Rezeption.

Gast:	1. möchte am nächsten Tag auschecken.
Rezeptionist/-in:	2. Rechnung wird vorbereitet; fragt nach Zahlungsart.
Gast:	3. mit Kreditkarte.
Rezeptionist/-in:	4. kein Problem.

Am nächsten Tag

Gast:	5. möchte die Rechnung haben.
Rezeptionist/-in:	6. händigt Rechnung aus.
Gast:	7. ist erstaunt: hat das eine Telefonat vorgestern bereits sofort bar bezahlt.
Rezeptionist/-in:	8. entschuldigt sich; zieht es von der Rechnung ab.
Gast:	9. übergibt seine Kreditkarte.
Rezeptionist/-in:	10. bedauert, dass *Bust-Finance-Card* nicht akzeptiert wird.
Gast:	11. was jetzt?
Rezeptionist/-in:	12. andere Kreditkarten?
Gast:	13. leider nicht; schlägt Barzahlung vor.
Rezeptionist/-in:	14. kein Problem.
Gast:	15. stellt fest, dass nicht genug Bargeld dabei; hat noch Schecks.
Rezeptionist/-in:	16. leider nicht; Reiseschecks wären möglich.
Gast:	17. erinnert sich, dass er noch einen hat.
Rezeptionist/-in:	18. kann den Rest ja damit bezahlen.
Gast:	19. ist erleichtert.

Complaints and Special Wishes in the Hotel

102

Ordnen Sie bitte die Nummern aus den Bildern M33/M34 den jeweiligen Begriffen zu und finden Sie die deutschen Ausdrücke.

Living Room/Bedroom	Nr.	Wohn-/Schlafraum
air conditioning		
alarm clock		
ashtray		
bed table		
carpet		
coat hanger		
coffee table		
curtain		
cushion		
desk		
double bed		
dressing table		
fireplace		
heating		
lamp		
mattress		
minibar		
mirror		
pillow		
quilt		
radiator		
reading lamp		
rug		
sheet		
single bed		
sofa/settee		
telephone		
thermostat		
trouser press		
TV/television		
twin bed		
wardrobe		
wastepaper basket		

Bathroom	Nr.	Badezimmer
cistern		
comb		
faucet/(BE) tap		
flannel		
garbage bin		
mirror		
plug		
(electric) razor		
razorblade		
shampoo		
shower		
soap		
socket		
sponge		
toilet		
toilet roll/paper		
toilet seat		
toothbrush		
toothpaste		
towel		
washbasin		

4268128

103

Unten sind Beispiele für einige Beschwerdegründe vorgegeben. Welche weiteren häufigen Beschwerden können sich im Zusammenhang mit den links aufgelisteten Gegenständen ergeben?

Words and phrases you might find helpful:
blocked
broken
dirty
empty
full
locked
missing
out of order
... doesn't work
... has not been cleaned
... has not been emptied
... has not been made
I can't find any ... in my room

104

Formulieren Sie jetzt bitte einige Beschwerden und die angemessenen Reaktionen darauf. Die Tabellen können Ihnen bei den Antworten behilflich sein.

Ein Gast ruft an der Rezeption mit einer Beschwerde an.

Gast: Excuse me, Miss, but the bed in my room has not been made.
Rezeptionistin: Oh, I'm awfully sorry, madam. I'll send someone up to make it at once.

I'm	very really	sorry, sorry to hear that,	madam. miss. sir.

<table>
<tr><td>I'll bring
I'll send</td><td>one
some</td><td colspan="3">for you</td><td rowspan="3">at once.
immediately.</td></tr>
<tr><td>I'll send
I'll ask</td><td>someone
the chambermaid
the ...</td><td>(up) to</td><td>change
fix
...</td><td>it
them</td></tr>
<tr><td colspan="5">I'll see to it</td></tr>
</table>

Complaints and Special Wishes in the Hotel

Bei der Ankunft äußert ein Gast an der Rezeption eine spezielle Bitte.

Gast:	I'm afraid I've forgotten to bring my soap! Could you get me some, please?
Rezeptionist/-in:	Certainly, miss, no problem. There is already a small cake in your bathroom, but I'll send you some extra ones.
Gast:	That's very kind. Thank you very much indeed.
Rezeptionist/-in:	You're welcome, miss.

105

Überlegen Sie sich bitte, welche Sonderwünsche ein Gast haben könnte.

• A stain on a blouse/shirt/skirt	→	Send it to a launderette
• Theater tickets for tomorrow night	→	Try to get some
• Flowers for a businessfriend's wife	→	Show way to flower shop
• An extra armchair for her/his room	→	Room too small
• A telephone/fax number	→	Look it up
• Departure time of plane/train	→	Give her/him a timetable
______	→	______
______	→	______
______	→	______
______	→	______
______	→	______
______	→	______
______	→	______
______	→	______
______	→	______
______	→	______
______	→	______
______	→	______
______	→	______

106

Formulieren Sie nun bitte einige Sonderwünsche und die angemessenen Reaktionen darauf. Auch hier kann Ihnen die Tabelle in Übung Nr. 104 einen Anhalt geben.

Words and phrases you might find helpful:	
telephone directory	I'm afraid, that's not possible, sir, because ...

4268130

„Ihr" Hotel hat eine Anfrage erhalten (→ M36). Sie werden gebeten diesen Brief mit einem deutschsprachigen Memo der Salesmanagerin zur Bearbeitung vorzulegen.

107

Schreiben Sie bitte die zur Bearbeitung der Anfrage benötigten Informationen heraus.

Memo

Auf der Grundlage Ihres Memos hat die Salesmanagerin, Meta Mustermann, ihrem Mitarbeiter Ole Olsen die Anfrage sowie die nachfolgend wiedergegebene Notiz auf den Schreibtisch gelegt.

- *Bitte Schreiben der Leatherstocking Inc. beantworten*
- *Übliche Antwort mit Hotelprospekt u. Preisliste*
- *Zusätzlich auf folgende Punkte hinweisen:*
  a) Preisnachlass von 15 % für Konferenzen mit mind. 50 Teilnehmern
  b) Angebot: 3 Mahlzeiten pro Tag für € 155,00 pro Person
  c) Möglichkeit zur Teilnahme am Musikfestival u. Galadiner

Mustermann

Correspondence: Offer

108

Ergänzen Sie gegebenenfalls diese Auflistung.

Some alternative phrases

a) we thank you for your letter dated August 16 concerning

- thank you very much for your letter dated
- we thank you for your letter of 16 August in which you
- we were pleased to receive your letter
- ______________________________
- ______________________________

b) we are looking forward to hearing from you soon

- please answer as soon as possible
- this offer is valid only until
- we would appreciate your rapid reply
- ______________________________
- ______________________________

c) we would like to submit the following offer

- we can make an offer under the following terms and conditions
- ______________________________
- ______________________________

d) ______________________________

- ______________________________
- ______________________________

4268132

„Ihr" Hotel hat ein Schreiben mit der folgenden Anfrage erhalten.

From 2nd till 14th November we would like to book rooms for fifteen members of our firm. In addition, we will need a conference room for the whole time, and for the last two days we would like to arrange an exhibition of our products for the German partners of our firm (a room of about 250 m^2 will be needed for that); enclosed please find for your information a brochure which shows a variety of our products.

As eight of us will be accompanied by wives or husbands, we would appreciate it if you could help organizing a program for their entertainment for some of the days during the time of our stay.

Please send us information about the prices of your meals, as we would like to take them individually according to our needs and likings.

109

Verfassen Sie unter Ihrem Namen ein Angebot – einen formal vollständigen Geschäftsbrief mit heutigem Datum – auf der Grundlage der folgenden Stichwörter als Antwort auf die oben stehende Anfrage. Bringen Sie die einzelnen Punkte in eine sinnvolle Reihenfolge.

Words and phrases you might find helpful:

p.d. = per day	at a total of
p.n. = per night	equipped with
p.p. = per person	facilities
to allow/to grant a reduction	latest technical equipment

Da für die infrage kommende Zeit Sonderaktionen geplant sind, können Sie der anfragenden Firma nicht wie üblich Hotelbroschüren schicken, sondern müssen die Einzelposten im Brief nennen.

Einzelzimmer: € 115,00 pro Nacht

Adresse: Renaissance, Ltd.
1 The Mall
London SW1
Great Britain

Ihre Sekretärin heißt: Marthe Schwerdtlein

Mittagessen: € 16,50 bis € 35,00

Programm für Ehepartner kann organisiert werden (Ausflüge, Besichtigungen, Einkaufsbummel u. Ä.)

Der Sekretär des Adressaten heißt: Ben Jonson

Kein Preisnachlass möglich

Konferenzraum für 15 Personen (modernste technische Ausstattung): € 210,00 pro Tag (reduzierter Sonderpreis!)

Frühstücksbüfett: € 13,00

Zweitägige Ausstellung der Produkte kann arrangiert werden; zwei miteinander verbundene Räume à 120 m^2 zu insgesamt € 500,00 pro Tag

Mittag- u. Abendessen: à la carte

Absender:
Haus zur Bruchbude
Sumpfgasse 123
45678 Kleinkleckersdorf

Abendessen: ab € 16,00

Verfasser der Anfrage ist:
Christopher Marlowe
Senior Executive Manager
Renaissance, Ltd.

Doppelzimmer: € 80,00 pro Person und Nacht

110

Ergänzen Sie gegebenenfalls diese Auflistung.

Some alternative phrases

a) which we hereby confirm

- herewith we confirm
- this is to confirm
- ______________________
  ____
  ____
- ______________________
  ____
  ____

b) we look forward to welcoming you in

- we are expecting you by August 3
- your rooms will be ready
- ______________________
  ____
  ____
- ______________________
  ____
  ____

c) any further wishes will find our careful attention

- please let us know if
- should any further wishes arise, please do not hesitate to contact us
- ______________________
  ____
- ______________________
  ____

d) ______________________
____
____
____

- ______________________
  ____
- ______________________
  ____

4268134

111

Ergänzen Sie gegebenenfalls diese Auflistung.

Some alternative phrases

a) may we draw your attention to the fact that

- may we remind you of our invoice
- as you have not yet settled our invoice we would like to
- ______________________________
- ______________________________

b) please see to this matter

- please settle the matter
- please make sure that
- ______________________________
- ______________________________

c) in the near future

- within the next few days
- by the end of August
- ______________________________
- ______________________________

Second reminder

d) as you disregarded our letter of May 27

- ______________________________

e) if you should also disregard this reminder we shall be forced to take legal action against you

- ______________________________

Correspondence: Refusal

Das Hotel „Haus zur Bruchbude" hat eine Anfrage erhalten (→ M41), der leider nicht entsprochen werden kann. Um jedoch einen möglicherweise guten Kunden nicht zu verlieren, macht das Salesoffice einen Gegenvorschlag (→ M42).

112

Ergänzen Sie gegebenenfalls diese Auflistung.

Some alternative phrases

a) as we are fully booked

- due to the fact that we are
- being outbooked we are not able to
- ______________________________
  ____
- ______________________________
  ____

b) we regret that we have to inform you

- we are sorry to say that
- ______________________________
  ____

c) we are in no position to carry out

- we are unable to execute
- ______________________________
  ____

d) we trust that our situation finds your kind understanding

- that this difficulty will not overshadow our good business relations
- we most sincerely hope that
- ______________________________
  ____
  ____
- ______________________________
  ____
  ____

e) ______________________________
____
____

- ______________________________
  ____
  ____

4268136

113

Schreiben Sie bitte zunächst Ihren Lebenslauf (komplett mit allen Daten und Fakten).

Curriculum Vitae

Name

Address

Telephone/Telefax

Date of Birth

Place of Birth

Nationality

Education

Qualifications

114

Verfassen Sie dann zur Übung zwei Bewerbungen:

- eine als direkte Antwort auf eine Anzeige,
- eine als „kalte Bewerbung", d. h. eine Bewerbung, ohne dass ein spezifisches Angebot vorliegt.

Nehmen Sie ein Hotel Ihrer Wahl oder greifen Sie auf die Betriebe zurück, die Sie in M49 erwähnt finden.

Advanced — Describing the Restaurant

Zu Werbezwecken möchten die Restaurants der Stadt, in der Sie arbeiten, eine mehrsprachige Informationsbroschüre herausgeben. Sie werden gebeten für „Ihr" Restaurant einen englischen Beitrag vorzubereiten.

115

Entscheiden Sie zunächst bitte, welche Informationen für Ihren Beitrag wichtig sind. Streichen Sie in der unten stehenden Liste Punkte, die nicht in Ihren Beitrag aufgenommen werden sollen, bzw. fügen Sie Ergänzungen hinzu.

Anzahl der Angestellten
Lage/Umgebung
Name des Küchenchefs
Restauranttyp
Name des Restaurants
Tätigkeitsbereiche der Angestellten
Einrichtung
Name des Besitzers
Anzahl der Plätze
Anfahrtsbeschreibung für Auto und/oder ÖPNV
Name des Geschäftsführers

____

____

____

____

____

____

____

116

Im Folgenden finden Sie Vokabeln bzw. Phrasen, die Ihnen helfen können „Ihr" Restaurant zu beschreiben. Ergänzen Sie diese Listen.

Location	is located/situated	in the neighborhood of
	overlooks	in the center
	near	on the outskirts
	... minutes from	peaceful
	on foot/by car, bus ...	restful

4268138

Surroundings		
	parks/woods	
	shopping area	
	(administration) offices	

Building		
	modern	old/listed building
	stylish	period
	fine/beautiful	half-timbered
		thatched
	big	
	extensive	

Furnishing/ Equipment		
	(fully) air-conditioned	wood-panelled
	furnished	
	styled	
	equipped with	

Service		
	attentive	friendly
	courteous	unobtrusive

Dealing with Guests in the Restaurant

Dieser Dialog findet in dem Restaurant eines Hotels früh am Morgen statt. Mrs Gibson, ein Stammgast, kommt von ihrem Zimmer, um das Frühstück einzunehmen.

117

Bitte ergänzen Sie die Redeanteile der Bedienung.

Bedienung: 1. ______________________________

Gast: Good morning. Thank you.

Bedienung: 2. ______________________________

Gast: Well, actually I didn't. I couldn't get any sleep because of a terrible headache.

Bedienung: 3. ______________________________

Gast: It's all my fault. I shouldn't have drunk so much of your marvellous "Altbier". Well, maybe a good breakfast will make up for that. What've you got?

Bedienung: 4. ______________________________

Gast: No thanks. I can't understand it anyway. Can you recommend anything light?

Bedienung: 5. ______________________________

Gast: No eggs, please. Oh, I know. First I'll have some cornflakes, with a lot of milk.

Bedienung: 6. ____

____

____

Gast: Of course. A big mug of it, please. This will probably save my life.

Bedienung: 7. ____

____

____

Einige Minuten später kehrt die Bedienung zurück.

Bedienung: 8. ____

____

____

Gast: Oh, thanks. That's exactly what I need right now.

Bedienung: 9. ____

____

____

Gast: Maybe a few slices of toast with jam. And after that we'll see if my stomach can stand anything else.

Bedienung: 10. ____

____

____

Nach einer Weile kommt die Bedienung mit einem Tablett zurück.

Bedienung: 11. ____

____

____

Gast: That's perfect, thank you.

Bedienung: 12. ______________________________

____

____

Mrs Gibson isst noch, als die Bedienung zurückkehrt.

Bedienung: 13. ______________________________

____

____

Gast: *Yes, thank you. I feel a lot better now. Could you bring me some of that dark bread you call "Schwarzbrot".*

Bedienung: 14. ______________________________

____

____

Gast: Maybe with some spicy cheese like Cheddar.

Bedienung: 15. ______________________________

____

____

Gast: OK, Dutch cheese then. And some more coffee please.

Bedienung: 16. ______________________________

____

____

4268142

Dealing with Guests in the Restaurant

118

Bitte finden Sie je zwei englische Umsetzungen zu jeder dieser Situationen.

Die Bedienung ...

1. ... fragt die Gäste, ob sie reserviert haben.
2. ... teilt mit, dass keine Tische mehr frei sind.
3. ... bittet die Gäste um ihre Garderobe.
4. ... führt die Gäste zu ihrem Tisch.
5. ... bietet den Gästen die Speisenkarte an.
6. ... empfiehlt Menü X.
7. ... rät von Gericht Y ab.
8. ... nimmt die Bestellung auf.
9. ... fragt, ob die Weinkarte gewünscht wird.
10. ... muss einen Wunsch ablehnen.
11. ... bringt das bestellte Essen.
12. ... erkundigt sich während des Essens, ob alles in Ordnung ist.
13. ... erwidert den Dank des Gastes.

119

Vergleichen Sie nun bitte in Ihrer Lerngruppe Ihre Lösungen und ergänzen Sie gegebenenfalls Ihre Liste.

120

Entwerfen Sie bitte für die unten stehend skizzierte Situation einen englischen Dialog. Dieser Dialog sollte alle Situationen umfassen, die sich von dem Moment an ergeben, wenn ein Gast das Restaurant betritt, bis hin zur Aufnahme der Bestellung.

Ein Englisch sprechender Gast betritt das Restaurant um 20:15 Uhr; er hat einen Platz reserviert.

Die Bedienung bringt ihm die Speisenkarte.

Die Bedienung erkundigt sich nach der Bestellung.

Der Gast hat Schwierigkeiten, die deutsche Speisenkarte zu lesen. Er erkundigt sich bei der Bedienung nach einem typisch deutschen Gericht.

Die Bedienung empfiehlt „Rinderbraten (roast beef) mit gemischtem Gemüse und Kartoffeln".

Der Gast lehnt ab; er möchte ein Gericht mit Bohnen.

Die Bedienung bietet ihm an, das gleiche Gericht statt mit gemischtem Gemüse nur mit Bohnen zu servieren.

Der Gast akzeptiert und fragt, ob dazu ein Bier passt.

Die Bedienung bestätigt und fragt, ob er „Pils" oder „Alt" bevorzugt.

Der Gast bestellt ein Pils.

Dealing with Guests in the Restaurant: Paying

121

Setzen Sie bitte die folgenden Sprechabsichten in einen englischen Dialog um.

Words and phrases you might find helpful:

cash	receipt
check, (BE) cheque	service (charge)
cover (charge)	tax
item	VAT = value added tax
major credit cards	

Nach dem Essen wendet sich ein Gast aus einer Gruppe Geschäftsleute an die Bedienung.

Gast:	1.	bittet die Bedienung um die Rechnung.
Bedienung:	2.	fragt, ob einzelne Rechnungen gewünscht werden oder ob der Gast für alle zahlt.
Gast:	3.	zahlt für alle.
Bedienung:	4.	fragt nach der Zahlungsart.
Gast:	5.	möchte bar zahlen.
Bedienung:	6.	?
Bedienung:	7.	händigt die Rechnung aus.
Gast:	8.	hat für eine so hohe Summe nicht genügend Bargeld dabei; fragt, ob auch Schecks akzeptiert werden.
Bedienung:	9.	verneint bedauernd; weist darauf hin, dass alle größeren Kreditkarten akzeptiert werden.
Gast:	10.	hat nur eine *Bust-Finance-Card*.
Bedienung:	11.	wird auch akzeptiert.
Gast:	12.	ist erleichtert; fragt, ob Steuer im Preis eingeschlossen ist.
Bedienung:	13.	bestätigt, dass Mehrwertsteuer und Bedienung eingeschlossen sind.
Gast:	14.	händigt seine Karte aus.
Bedienung:	15.	bittet um einen Moment Geduld.
Bedienung:	16.	übergibt Karte und Quittung.
Gast:	17.	bedankt sich; hat noch eine Frage.
Bedienung:	18.	?
Gast:	19.	möchte wissen, was der erste Punkt auf der Rechnung bedeutet.
Bedienung:	20.	erklärt, was ein Couvert ist und dass es zum Verzehrten addiert wird.
Gast:	21.	bedankt sich für die Auskunft; gibt Trinkgeld für sehr guten Service.
Bedienung:	22.	bedankt sich ausdrücklich; wünscht einen guten Tag.

4268144

Sie machen Ihre Ausbildung in einem Familienbetrieb, der eine etwas fantasielose Speisenkarte mit Gerichten der gutbürgerlichen Art bietet (→ M17). Sie bekommen den Auftrag, die Karte zu übersetzen.

122

Überlegen Sie bitte, ob Sie unter Umständen einiges erklären müssen (z. B. „Berliner Art", „Eisbein", „Rote Grütze" u. Ä.).

Words and phrases you might find helpful:

broth	preservative
coloring	sweetener
cream of ... soup	to thicken
custard	

123

Finden Sie bitte englische Entsprechungen für die links unten aufgeführten Begriffe, die Ihnen in der folgenden Übung eine Hilfe sein können.

abgestimmt	______________________
ausgewogen	______________________
bckömmlich	______________________
blau, blutig (Steak)	______________________
dettig	______________________
englisch (Steak)	______________________
erfrischend	______________________
gesund	______________________
gut durch gebraten/gegrillt	______________________
gut gewürzt	______________________
herzhaft	______________________
kalorienreich	______________________
knackig	______________________
knusprig	______________________
lecker, schmackhaft	______________________
mager	______________________
pikant	______________________
sättigend	______________________
scharf	______________________
weich	______________________
wie bei Muttern	______________________
würzig	______________________
zart	______________________

Ein Gast sitzt offensichtlich etwas hilflos vor einer Speisenkarte, die ein Betrieb der gehobenen Gastronomie seinen Gästen „zumutet" (→ M18 – M22), und bittet Sie ihm einiges zu erklären.

124

Versuchen Sie bitte sechs dieser Gerichte (sowie den Zusatz auf der Fischkarte) einem Gast, der Deutsch nur teilweise lesen kann, zu ERKLÄREN – NICHT ZU ÜBERSETZEN. Überlegen Sie sich zunächst, welche Informationen der Gast wirklich benötigt, um sinnvoll eine Wahl treffen zu können, und formulieren Sie dann mit Ihren eigenen Worten auf Englisch. Zur Erinnerung: bitte keine Übersetzung! Als Anregung finden Sie hier das Beispiel „Gefüllte Tomaten".

Words and phrases you might find helpful:

bitter	rare	well seasoned
egg white	raw	whipped cream
finger biscuits	salty	
hot	selection	we serve ... with ...
light	sweet	it is served on ...
medium	well done	it's a combination of ... and ...

Gefüllte Tomaten

Wir servieren Ihnen zarteste Freilandtomaten mit einer fein abgestimmten Füllung aus köstlichen Bananen, fruchtiger Ananas und einer Mischung erlesener Nüsse. Abgerundet wird diese Komposition von einer mit ein wenig Zitrone aromatisierten erfrischenden Creme.

€ 10,00

(fresh) tomatoes
stuffed with
bananas/pineapples
(mixed) nuts
fresh lemon cream

Gast: Excuse me, Miss, I understand *Tomaten*, *Bananen*, *Ananas* and all that stuff alright, but I can't make anything of the rest. Could you please explain what all this rigmarole means?

Bedienung: Well, sir, *gefüllte Tomaten* are tomatoes stuffed with a mixture of, as you said, bananas, pineapples and nuts with a fresh lemon cream. It's very nice, indeed.

4268146

125

Entwickeln Sie nun bitte einen Dialog auf der Grundlage der Speisenkarte M23, der die unten angeführten Sprechabsichten von Gast und Bedienung auf Englisch umsetzt.

Gast:

You have taken a seat at a table in a restaurant.

You don't speak German, so you hardly understand anything that you see on the menu.

The time is about noon and you don't have too much time for your lunch.

You are thinking about a soup or a hot starter.

You don't like poultry.

Let the waitress/waiter explain to you, what *Geschnetzeltes Schweinefilet in Gorgonzolarahm mit Gemüsebukett und Kartoffelkroketten* is. After she/he did so you decide you don't like it and let her/him recommend something else. You follow the recommendation.

You would like mineral water with the meal.

At first you don't intend to take a dessert, but when the waitress/waiter recommends the one with cherries, you make up your mind.

Bedienung:

Ein Gast hat an einem Tisch Platz genommen und möchte zu Mittag essen. Sie begrüßen ihn zunächst auf Deutsch, stellen aber fest, dass der Gast nur Englisch spricht.

Sie fragen, ob der Gast ein 3-Gang-Menü wünscht oder nur einen Hauptgang.

Sie fragen, welches Getränk der Gast wünscht.

Sie beantworten die Fragen des Gastes hinsichtlich der Karteneinträge.

Vom Küchenchef wissen Sie, dass die Gerichte mit Ente verkauft werden müssen. Also beginnen Sie mit Ihren Empfehlungen bei diesen Gerichten.

Sie versuchen dem Gast ein Dessert schmackhaft zu machen. Sie beginnen dabei mit dem warmen Apfelkuchen.

Words and phrases you might find helpful:

caramel	marinated/pickled
clear soup/consommé	ragout/stew
flambé/flambéed	sherbet/sorbet
gratinated/au gratin	snails

126

Führen Sie nun Rollenspiele mit der Karte M23 durch. Gehen Sie aber zunächst die Karte auf eventuelle sprachliche Unklarheiten durch.

International Food

Sie geraten mit einem ausländischen Gast in ein Gespräch über die Küche seines Landes. Er zeigt ein sehr großes Interesse an diesem Thema und möchte nun seinerseits informiert werden über das, was typisch ist für die deutsche Küche.

127

Notieren Sie sich nun bitte zunächst in Stichworten Fakten über die deutsche Küche im Allgemeinen bzw. die spezielle Küche Ihrer Heimatregion.

128

Versuchen Sie dann bitte mithilfe dieser Stichwörter Eigenheiten der deutschen Küche (keine Gerichte!), ähnlich wie in den übrigen Artikeln über *International Food*, **mündlich** zu beschreiben.

Ein ausländischer Gast, der Deutsch nur unzureichend oder gar nicht spricht, sitzt in „Ihrem" Restaurant und möchte von Ihnen bei der Auswahl seines Essens beraten werden.

129 Wählen Sie zunächst eine Nationalität aus. Erkundigen Sie sich höflich und diskret, ob bzw. welche Ernährungsregeln der Gast befolgt, und beraten Sie ihn dann auf der Grundlage der Artikel über *International Food.*

Words and phrases you might find helpful:

basically	it is made from ...
mainly	it is made with ...
variety	it is served with ...
	you eat it with ...

Darüber hinaus erkundigt der Gast sich auch nach Gerichten, die „typisch deutsch" bzw. typisch für „Ihre" Region sind.

130 Die folgenden Beispiele sollen Ihnen hierfür Anregungen geben.

Himmel un Ääd (Himmel und Erde; rheinisch)
Oh, that's quite a simple dish from the Rhine area, madam. It's basically mashed potatoes with apple sauce, which sometimes is mixed with the mashed potatoes but here you get it as a side dish. With it we serve fried black pudding – which is made mainly from pig's blood – and some fried onions. It's really lovely. (You see, the name means "heaven and earth", and refers to the fact that the potatoes are taken from the soil and the apples from the opposite direction, the heaven).

Labskaus (norddeutsch)
That's a meal from northern Germany. It's a mixture of corned meat, mashed potatoes and beetroot, which you sometimes get as an extra on the side. We serve it with a sour herring and a fried egg. I'm afraid it's not up to everyone's taste, but personally I love it.

Quarkkäulchen (sächsisch)
They are a special kind of Saxonian dessert. You fry little cakes made mainly of mashed potatoes, curd, eggs, flour and raisins. We serve them either with custard or sugar and cinnamon or vanilla ice-cream and cherries. Whatever you may prefer, sir.

Käsefondue (schweizerisch)
Swiss specialty: melted Swiss cheese (Gruyère), Swiss wine, garlic and cherry brandy, bread-cubes, with special, long forks.

Maultaschen (schwäbisch/badisch)
German kind of pasta, ground beef, in broth, sometimes meat with spinach.

Kaiserschmarren (österreichisch)
Sweet pancake, little pieces, very rich.

Oder Dampfnudel oder Leberknödel oder Saumagen oder Thüringer Klöße oder ... oder ... oder ...

Wine

Wein ist festgelegt als Erzeugnis, das ausschließlich durch vollständige oder teilweise alkoholische Gärung der frischen, auch eingemaischten Weintrauben oder des Traubenmostes gewonnen wird. Weine aus anderen Früchten müssen nach der Frucht benannt sein, aus der sie bereitet wurden (z. B. Apfelwein, Kirschwein usw.).

131

Versuchen Sie bitte auf Englisch zu erklären, was Wein ist.

Words and phrases you might find helpful:

alcohol	grape
alcoholic	mash
to ferment	to mash
fermentation	must

132

Suchen Sie bitte die englischen Entsprechungen aus diesem Text für die nachfolgend aufgelisteten Begriffe heraus.

Wine, as you have seen in the short passage above, is made of the grapes taken from a vine. The place where the grapes are grown is called a vineyard and the place where they make wine is called a winery. In the French Champagne district for instance a lot of the champagne firms do not own vinyards (or at least not large or many vineyards) but they have presses, cellars, tanks, casks etc. On the other hand, the vinyardists (i.e. the "wine-farmers") of that region do not have the facilities to make champagne; they only sell their harvest to the champagne producers. The equivalent for the French château, i.e. a place where both is done – growing vines and making wine –, is called an estate. Champagne, by the way, is a sparkling wine, whereas claret is a still red wine from the area of Bordeaux. Another famous French wine is Burgundy. Well-known German white wines are Rhine wine and Moselle (this word can stand for the wine as well as the river or the whole area). There is no English word for a wine whose color is between red and white: it is called a rosé. Quite popular all over the world are two fortified wines from Spain and Portugal, viz. sherry and port.

An obstacle that has to be removed before you can savor your wine is the cork in the neck of the bottle. A corkscrew is quite helpful for that purpose. A special instrument used by waitresses and waiters is called "waiter's friend" (even if a waitress uses it). After opening the bottle (hopefully, you have not forgotten to let the guest have a look at the label) wines with a lot of sediment have to be decanted. But please, never, never put the decanter into a wine bucket. A champagne bucket is what you use in order to keep cool a bottle of champagne or only a bottle of plain sparkling wine.

4268150

aufgespriteter Wein	
(roter) Bordeaux	
Burgunder	
Champagner	
dekantieren	
Etikett	
Karaffe	
Kellnermesser	
Korken	
Korkenzieher	
Mosel(wein)	
Portwein	
Rheinwein	
Rosé	
Rotwein	
Sekt/Schaumwein	
Sektkühler	
Sherry	
Wein	
Weinstock/-pflanze	
Weinberg/-gut	
Weinkühler	
Weißwein	

133

Versuchen Sie bitte die Bedeutung des Wortes *„hock"* herauszufinden.

Beim Verkosten eines Weins müssen Sie die Kategorien Aussehen, Geruch und Geschmack beurteilen.

134

Fertigen Sie bitte eine Liste für die Beschreibung von Weinen an mit den in den folgenden Artikeln genannten Begriffen. Fügen Sie dieser Liste noch weitere Ausdrücke hinzu, die Sie für sinnvoll halten. Die unten aufgeführten Begriffe sollen eine Anregung bieten.

Abgang
Angriff
flach
fruchtig
geschmacklos
glänzend
hell
klar

Körper
körperreich
-lich (z. B. grün**lich**)
ölig (dick)
rau
reif
samtig
schwach

stark
Süße
Tannin (Gerbsäure)
tanninhaltig
trüb
vollmundig

Wine

Wein wird auf allen Kontinenten produziert (nun gut: **nicht** *in der Antarktis). Hier sind einige Informationen über englischsprachige Länder und die dort hergestellten Weine:*

USA

California is the main wine-producing region. Many of the best wines are made north of San Francisco in the Napa Valley. The Cabernet Sauvignon and Pinot Noir are important for the production of red wines, and the Chardonnay and Sauvignon for whites. The Zinfandel is a black grape peculiar to California which produces full-bodied wines with rich fruit flavours. Medium-bodied reds are made from the Gamay. Some wines are labelled Gamay Beaujolais, after a new type of grape variety. The Californian Sauvignons differ from their European counterparts by being lower in acidity which makes them fuller and 'grapier'. The fullbodied Chardonnays are usually good quality wines. Johannisberg Riesling can be dry to sweet, but because Californian wines are softer than their European counterparts, a medium sweet label may seem sweeter than say a Riesling Kabinett from the Mosel-Saar-Ruwer in Germany. Many Cabernet Sauvignons have proved to age well.

South Africa

The heart of the wine-growing region is Paarl, at the southern tip of the African continent. Other important regions include Stellenbosch, Constantia and Tullbagh. Along this part of the coast, the climate is ideal for wine growing having no extremes of temperature or rainfall. White wines are made from Chenin Blanc (Steen), Sémillon, Rhine Riesling, Palomino and Colombard, and red from Cabernet Sauvignon and Pinotage. Rieslings are dry and fresh, but usually unlike German Rieslings. The Chenin Blanc nearly always has a hint of sweetness, sometimes with a honey flavour. The Grunberger Stein, mainly from Chenin Blanc, has a refreshing tang to it.

New Zealand

The climate, particularly on North Island, is ideally suited to the production of light, elegant white wines, with cooling breezes from the ocean and mountains, high rainfall and morning mist. White grape varieties grown are Chardonnay, Gewürztraminer and Sauvignon. Good red wines – harder to find - are made from Cabernet Sauvignon and Pinot Noir.

Australia

Most Australian wine is produced in the states of South Australia, New South Wales and Victoria which lie between the latitudes 32° and 38°. Increasing amounts are being produced in Western Australia, and a small amount in Queensland and Tasmania. Being in the southern hemisphere, the vintage takes place between January and May. The main grape varieties are Sémillon (sometimes called Hunter Riesling), Rhine Riesling, Chardonnay, Gewürztraminer, Chenin Blanc, Muscat and Sauvignon for white wines, and Cabernet Sauvignon, Syrah (Shiraz), Merlot and Malbec for reds. Several producers from the Barossa Valley make good Germantype whites. Hill-Smith, Kaiser Stuhl and Orlando-Gramp produce a range from dry to late-picked, and much sweeter still. Good red wines from the Syrah grape are also made in the Barossa Valley.

Some of the finest dry whites in Australia are made from the Sémillon grape by the Rothbury Estate, Tulloch and Tyrell in the Hunter Valley. These have been compared to the great Graves of France, and improve with age. Chardonnays also from the Hunter Valley are remarkable for their full flavour.

aus: Jennifer Murray, Servicecraft. Wine Service Workbook, Macmillan Education Ltd, Basingstoke/London 1991

135 Bitte verfassen Sie – mithilfe der Fachliteratur ihrer Schule – einen ähnlichen Artikel über Weine aus dem UK.

4268152

Für die englischsprachige Weinkarte Ihres Betriebes sollen Sie die dort aufgeführten Weine kurz beschreiben. Sie informieren sich in der Fachliteratur und finden die folgenden Charakterisierungen.

1. Die goldgelbe Farbe dieses Weins aus dem Jahr 1987 verliert ein bisschen durch einen leichten Stich ins Grünliche. Man wird jedoch entschädigt durch eine fruchtige Nase sowie im Geschmack durch die angenehme Säure, die an Äpfel und Ananas erinnert.
2. Dieser goldfarbene 1984er ist im Bukett von einer säuerlichen Frische, die sich auf der Zunge bestätigt. Im Ganzen zeigt er sich jedoch überraschend harmonisch und ausgewogen.
3. Dieser 1985er von einem der berühmtesten Weingüter besticht durch eine tiefrote Farbe, die an den Rändern zu Orange verblasst. Er weist eine feine, fruchtige Nase auf und erinnert im Geschmack deutlich an reife Erdbeeren.
4. Dieser rote Bordeaux aus dem Jahr 1982 präsentiert sich in einem funkelnden, tiefen Rubinrot. Das Bukett weist Anklänge an Kirschen und dunkle Beeren auf. Am Gaumen sind deutlich Tannine wahrnehmbar sowie Anklänge an Holz. Am eindrucksvollsten jedoch ist sein phänomenal langer Abgang.

136

Notieren Sie sich bitte die wichtigsten Stichwörter dieser Weinansprachen. Versuchen Sie dann die Weine auf Englisch zu beschreiben (keine Übersetzung!).

Words and phrases you might find helpful:

acidity	to fade	touch
balance	nose	vintage
claret	on the palate	vinyard

	Year	Look	Smell	Taste	Others
1.					
2.					
3.					
4.					

Beer

Für eine Spezialitätenwoche zum Thema „Bier" hat „Ihr" Betrieb für seine Gäste den Besuch einer Brauerei organisiert. Da nicht Deutsch sprechende Ausländer in der Gruppe sind, werden Sie gebeten die Führung zu begleiten und diesen Gästen mit englischen Erklärungen zu helfen.

137

Unten sind die wichtigsten Schritte der Bierherstellung aufgelistet. Suchen Sie sich bitte zunächst das Ihnen unbekannte englische Vokabular und beschreiben Sie dann – kurz, aber präzise – diesen Prozess.

Gerste/Weizen/Roggen	• in Wasser einweichen (und erwärmen) • keimt • darren → **Malz**
Malz	• schroten • mit Wasser mischen • erhitzen → **Maische**
Maische	• filtern → **Würze** und **Treber (Viehfutter)**
Würze	• **Hopfen** hinzufügen • kochen • kühlen • **Hefe** hinzufügen • gärt • filtern → **Bier**

Im Rahmen der Spezialitätenwoche „Bier" bietet „Ihr" Betrieb auch einige internationale Biere vom Fass. Da sich Ihre Englischkenntnisse bereits bei der Brauereiführung bestens bewährt haben, bekommen Sie den Auftrag, ein englisch-deutsches Informationsblatt über Biere deutsch- und englischsprachiger Länder zu erstellen. In der einschlägigen Fachliteratur finden Sie folgende Informationen.

138

Notieren Sie sich bitte die wichtigsten Stichwörter aus diesen Beiträgen und versuchen Sie dann mit ihrer Hilfe diese Biere auf Deutsch bzw. Englisch zu beschreiben (keine Übersetzung!).

The most fashionable brews in some parts of the United States, especially the West Coast, are a new generation of ales. These are often distinguished by an intensely floral hop character, featuring the varieties grown in Oregon and Washington states, and a fresh, assertive palate. Such ales are ideal partners to the new American cuisine.

Australia may be famous for standard lager, but there is more tingling refreshment in a glass of supposedly sparkling ale, the country's own contribution to the world of beer styles.

The great dry stouts are brewed in Ireland, and are instantly recognizable in their black creaminess. They are famously sociable brews, lubricating wit, music and literary tribute. They also have the stinging intensity of an amontillado sherry. By no means every glass of dry stout is served with oysters or lobster, but that is a marriage made in heaven.

Bitter is the principal style of ale sold in Britain, ideally enjoyed freshly drawn from the cask, in a pub, with friends. If a sociable evening is planned, devotees prefer a bitter that is low in gravity and alcohol. A good hop character is of the first importance, but beyond that it is a very wide-ranging style.

In the British Isles, porter came to mean a roasty, black, top-fermented brew that was a lighter-bodied counterpart to stout. It need not necessarily also be lower in alcohol. Porter went through a period of decline, vanished altogether from its native islands, then returned to become a style newly fashionable among lovers of flavorful beers. New-generation porters are also being widely produced in North America.

Altbier heißt das kupferfarbene, herbe, obergärige Bier aus Norddeutschland – am besten schmeckt es in den gemütlichen Gastwirtschaften Düsseldorfs. Seine reinmalzige Milde und sein Hopfencharakter werden durch kühle Reifung schön abgerundet.

Kölns Bier – hell wie Pilsner, aber so fruchtig wie Ale – besitzt eine ihm ganz eigene, verlockende Delikatesse. Kann irgendein anderes Bier gleichzeitig als Aperitif und Digestif fungieren?

Ob es nun der Name erkennen lässt oder nicht, die meisten Biere der Welt sind helle Lagerbiere des Pilsner Typs, die das große böhmische Original mehr oder weniger getreulich nachahmen. Ein Pilsner ist jedoch mehr als nur ein helles Bier. Der echte Pilsner Stil zeigt Malzcharakter, ist aber in der Blumigkeit des Aromas und der Herbheit im Abgang hopfenbetont.

Berliner Weiße wirkt herrlich durstlöschend, etwa so wie frisch gepresster Zitronensaft am Mittelmeer oder Limonensaft in Florida. Für manchen Geschmack aber ist sie zu sauer, und deshalb ist es Brauch geworden, einen Schuss Himbeersirup oder Waldmeisteraroma hineinzugeben.

Süddeutsches Weizenbier ist vor allem ein Sommergetränk. Es ist leicht und schäumend, hat die fruchtige Säure von Äpfeln und Pflaumen und erinnert oft an Gewürznelken. Klar oder naturtrüb, dunkel oder hell setzt es sich inzwischen überall in der Welt durch.

englische Texte aus: Michael Jackson, Beer Companion, Mitchell Beazley, London 1993)

deutsche Texte aus: Michael Jackson, Bier International, Hallwag, Bern/Stuttgart 1994

Cocktails

Ein schottischer Gast ist ganz begeistert von einem Cocktail, den Sie ihm gemacht haben, und möchte nun wissen, was er alles enthält und wie er gemacht wird.

139

Vervollständigen Sie bitte die folgende Rezeptur.

Words and phrases you might find helpful:

bar spoon	mixing glass	measure	to pass through
cocktail stick	sequence	• dash	to sieve
crushed ice	sieve	• one quarter/three quarters	to squeeze
ice cubes	strainer	• one fifth	to stir
ingredients	whisk	• liter/centiliter/milliliter	to strain
liquid			to whisk

Bobby Burns

1/2 Scotch Whisky
1/2 Vermouth rosso
3 Tropfen Benedictine
Zitronen- bzw. Orangenschale

Die Zutaten werden in der oben genannten Reihenfolge in ein vorgekühltes Mixglas gegeben. Die Mixtur wird umgerührt und in ein Cocktailglas gegossen. Abschließend wird über dem Getränk die Zitronen- bzw. Orangenschale ausgedrückt.

"Well, sir, it's quite simple in fact. First fill the following ______________________ into a cold ______________________; but make sure you do it exactly in this sequence: one half of Scotch Whisky, one half of Vermouth rosso and ______________________ of Bénédictine. ______________________ the liquid and ______________________ it into a glass. Finally ______________________ some lemon or orange peel over the cocktail. That's it. Cheerio!"

140

Versuchen Sie nun bitte das Rezept für *Grand Slam* wie oben zu beschreiben.

Grand Slam

1/2 Schwedenpunsch
1/4 Vermouth rosso
1/4 Vermouth dry

Die Zutaten werden in einem Shaker mit Eiswürfeln geschüttelt und dann in ein Cocktailglas abgeseiht.

Breakfast products	Nr.	Frühstückswaren
bacon		
cereal		
• cornflakes		
• granola		
• oatmeal		
cheese		
coffee		
• decaffeinated		
cold cuts		
croissant		
egg		
• boiled		
• fried		
• poached		
• scrambled		
• sunny-side-up		
ham		
hash browns		
hot chocolate		
maple syrup		
milk		
• skim milk		
omelette		
orange juice		
pancake		
preserve		
• jam		
• jelly		
• marmalade		
• honey		
tea		
waffle		

141

Ordnen Sie bitte die Nummern aus den Bildern M26/M27 den jeweiligen Begriffen zu und finden Sie die deutschen Ausdrücke.

Breakfast utensils	Nr.	Gerätschaften für das Frühstück
bread basket		
breakfast cup		
butter dish		
butter knife		
coffee pot		
egg-cup		
milk jug		
napkin		
preserve dish		
saucer		
side knife		
side plate		
spoon		
sugar bowl		
tea pot		
tea spoon		
toast rack		
tray		

Complaints and Special Wishes in the Restaurant

Ein Gast ruft einen Kellner und bringt eine Beschwerde vor.

Gast:	Excuse me, sir, my coffee is only lukewarm.
Bedienung:	Oh I'm awfully sorry. I'll bring you a new one in a second. I do apologize for that.

Beim Frühstück wendet sich ein Gast mit einer speziellen Bitte an eine Kellnerin.

Gast:	Excuse me, I'm a diabetic and I'm not supposed to have any sugar in my coffee. Could you get me some sweetener?
Bedienung:	Certainly, miss, no problem. I'll bring you some immediately.
Gast:	That's very kind. Thank you very much indeed.
Bedienung:	You're welcome, miss.

142

Formulieren Sie jetzt bitte einige Beschwerden bzw. Sonderwünsche und versuchen Sie dabei verschiedene Grade der Höflichkeit auszudrücken. Wie würden Sie in den einzelnen Fällen reagieren? Im Folgenden finden Sie einige Anregungen.

Words and phrases you might find helpful:

Complaints/Whishes	**Reactions**	
burnt/spoilt dirty/chipped missing/broken oversalted/tasteless	terribly/very to ask/to send someone to change/to clean	• I'll be with you in a moment.
I can't find any ... Is there no ...?	immediately/right away	• I'll see to it at once.
buffet	chef manager	• I'm afraid that's not possible because ...

Excuse me, miss, but I'm afraid I ordered some orange juice about twenty minutes ago.

Oh no, I explicitly ordered my scrambled eggs without herbs.

Waitress, there's no way I can eat this porridge; it's absolutely terrible.

I refuse to drink from a glass as dirty as that!

Hey, how the hell do you think I can drink this diafuckingbolic tea; it's as cold as a bloody iceberg.

4268158

„Ihr" Hotel möchte sich mit einer Seite im Internet präsentieren. Das Salesoffice bekommt von der Hotelleitung den Auftrag, einen Textentwurf für den Interneteintrag vorzubereiten. Als Mitarbeiter in diesem Team sind Sie dafür zuständig, einen solchen Entwurf auf Englisch zu präsentieren.

143

Zur Vorbereitung Ihrer Arbeit besorgen Sie sich bitte zunächst Hotelbroschüren, -prospekte u. Ä. und analysieren ihren Inhalt. Streichen Sie aus der folgenden Auflistung die Stichpunkte, die Ihnen unwichtig erscheinen, und ergänzen Sie gegebenenfalls Fehlendes. Tragen Sie dann die Stichwörter in die Liste auf der rechten Seite in der Reihenfolge ein, in der sie in Ihrer Broschüre erscheinen sollen.

leisure facilities
address
type of hotel
conference facilities
banqueting facilities
prices
number of staff
location
surroundings
special services
restaurant (type, size ...)
name of general manager
accessibility (by car, train, plane ...)
building (size, style, period ...)

Describing the Hotel

144

Tragen Sie bitte die jeweilige deutsche Übersetzung für die einzelnen Hotelbezeichnungen sowie die Nummern der entsprechenden Definitionen in die Tabelle ein.

Deutsche Hotelbezeichnung	Englische Hotelbezeichnung	Definition Nr.
	B & B	
	business hotel	
	boarding house	
	conference hotel	
	country house hotel	
	guest house	
	hostel	
	inn	
	luxury hotel	
	motel	
	resort hotel	
	spa hotel	
	sports hotel	

1. A hotel that provides as a special service treatments for ailments and diseases
2. A hotel which caters for the special needs of businessmen and -women
3. A hotel with furnishing, equipment and service of the highest level
4. A hotel on a somewhat smaller scale – mostly privately owned – which very often provides a personal and informal atmosphere
5. A kind of hotel which has been installed in a luxurious house in the country and which offers accommodation on a higher level
6. A hotel that offers parking place very often directly in front of the guest's room; in countries where people drive long distances
7. A hotel which offers facilities designed especially to answer to the needs of tourists
8. A hotel that has all the necessary facilities for any kind of meeting (business or otherwise)
9. A pub – usually in the countryside – that offers a few rooms as accommodation
10. A hotel with all the necessary facilities for certain kinds of sport
11. A hotel or guest house – sometimes even only one or two rooms in a private house – where the only meal on offer is breakfast
12. A kind of hotel which offers accommodation for a longer period of time so people can live there and do not stay only a few nights
13. A "hotel" that offers cheap accommodation and meals, very often for special groups of guests: youth ~, students' ~ etc.

4268160

145

Im Folgenden finden Sie Vokabeln bzw. Phrasen, die Ihnen helfen können „Ihr" Hotel zu beschreiben. Ergänzen Sie diese Listen.

Location	is located/situated	in the neighborhood of
	overlooks	in the center
	near	on the outskirts
	... minutes from	peaceful
	on foot/by car, bus ...	restful

Surroundings	central station/airport ...	parks/woods
	museums/theaters ...	shopping area
	churches	(administration) offices

Building	old/listed building	fine/beautiful
	modern	
	stylish	
		big
		extensive
	period	

Describing the Hotel

Rooms		
	single/double/twin room	(fully) air-conditioned
	suite/junior suite	furnished
	penthouse	styled
	connecting rooms	equipped with
	central heating	
		wood-panelled

Facilities		
	ambience	multigym
	amenity	whirlpool/jacuzzi
		indoor/outdoor pool
	conservatory	
	audio/video system	
	slide projection system	golf course
	public address system	tennis court

Service		
	attentive	friendly
	courteous	unobtrusive

Giving Directions

Ein Gast hat soeben eingecheckt und durch Zufall haben Sie keine englischen Broschüren mit Informationen über das Hotel zur Hand, so dass Sie ihm auf seine Fragen hin die örtlichen Gegebenheiten erklären müssen.

146 Bitte formulieren Sie zu den unten genannten Punkten – auf der Grundlage des Hotelplans M31 – sowohl die Fragen des Gastes als auch Ihre Antworten.

Frühstück	• Im „Restaurant an der Ecke" • Von 07:30 bis 10:30 Uhr • Büfett € 15,50
ÖPNV	• Haltestelle vom Ausgang nach rechts • 5 Minuten Fußweg • 12 Minuten Fahrt zur Messe mit Bus 68 • 17 Minuten zum Stadtzentrum mit Straßenbahn 34
Restaurants	• „Restaurant an der Ecke": typisch regionale Gerichte • „Gartenrestaurant": internationale Küche auf hohem Niveau
Zimmerservice	• Telefonnummer: 123
Buchhandlung	• In der Ladenpassage • Geöffnet zu üblichen Öffnungszeiten
Umgebung des Hotels	• Großzügige Parkanlage hinter dem Haus
Der Gast hat Durst	• Bar unmittelbar gegenüber der Rezeption

Words and phrases you might find helpful:

bus ride	multigym	streetcar/(BE) tram
cloakroom	next to	surroundings
elevator/(BE) lift	opening hours	toilet
extensive	park grounds	• comfort room, "CR"
facilities	public transport	• gentlemen's room
"haute cuisine"	sauna	• ladies' room
level	shopping gallery	• rest room

Giving Directions

Ein Gast wendet sich an Sie als Rezeptionist/-in, weil er fremd in der Stadt ist und eine bestimmte Adresse sucht.

147

Nehmen Sie nun bitte einen Stadtplan Ihrer Stadt und erklären Sie die Wege von dem Hotel, in dem Sie Ihre Ausbildung machen, zu verschiedenen markanten Punkten der Stadt. Die folgende Auflistung soll Ihnen einige Anregungen geben.

- Bahnhof
- Flughafen
- Geschäftszentren
  - Banken
  - Versicherungen
  - Fabriken
  - ...
- Einkaufszentren
- Restaurants
- Sehenswürdigkeiten
  - Nähere Ausflugsziele
  - Gebäude
  - Museen
  - Plätze
  - Parks
  - ...
- Sportstätten

Words and phrases you might find helpful:

go straight on	alley	factory
turn right/left (into ...)	avenue	golf course
	brewery	level crossing
cross *Hauptstraße*	car park	main station
go along *Fürstenwall*	• multi storey car park	pedestrians' area
turn into *Friedrichstraße*	• underground car park	pedestrians' crossing
	cathedral	shopping mall
after the department store	cemetery	stadium
at the traffic light	church	subway/(BE) underground
behind the theater	• Anglican church	taxi stand
on the corner	• Catholic church	tennis court
on the right/left (side)	• Protestant church	theater/(BE) theatre
	exposition/fair ground	theme park

4268164

Dieser Dialog findet in einem Hotel um 16:00 Uhr statt. Sie stehen an der Rezeption und Mrs Gibson, ein Stammgast, betritt die Hotelhalle.

148

Bitte ergänzen Sie die Redeanteile der Rezeptionistin bzw. des Rezeptionisten.

Rezeptionist/-in: 1.

Gast: Hi, here I am again. Long time no see. How've ye b'n doin'?

Rezeptionist/-in: 2.

Gast: Oh, sorry. I said, how have you been doing?

Rezeptionist/-in: 3.

Gast: Well, I'm fine, as long as I get a chance to travel.

Rezeptionist/-in: 4.

Gast: That's true. It's been almost eight months.

Rezeptionist/-in: 5.

Gast: Yes, I have. Can I have my regular room?

Rezeptionist/-in: 6. ______________________

____

____

Gast: Oh, certainly. It doesn't have to be the same one, as long as it's away from the street. And it's the same price, isn't it?

Rezeptionist/-in: 7. ______________________

____

____

Gast: That's good. At least that hasn't changed. You're still the most expensive place in town.

Rezeptionist/-in: 8. ______________________

____

____

Gast: No, no, just kiddin'.

Rezeptionist/-in: 9. ______________________

____

____

Gast: Yes, exactly. But I might be leaving a little bit earlier this time. I'd like to be back in New York, when my daughter has her birthday party.

Rezeptionist/-in: 10. ______________________

____

____

Gast: Good. This time I've got a lot of baggage. Can you call the porter please?

Rezeptionist/-in: 11. ______________________

____

____

4268166

Gast: So I won't have to wait here and can go right up to my room.

Rezeptionist/-in: 12. ______________________________

____

____

Gast: Don't worry. I've been here quite a few times before, remember? I don't suppose you've changed the elevator to the other side of the building.

Rezeptionist/-in: 13. ______________________________

____

____

Gast: Thanks a lot. Oh, by the way, can I get a meal right now, or is your restaurant closed for the afternoon?

Rezeptionist/-in: 14. ______________________________

____

____

Gast: Yes, would you please do that. You know the food on the plane was horrible again. I didn't touch a thing.

Nach einigen kurzen Augenblicken:

Rezeptionist/-in: 15. ______________________________

____

____

Gast: Oh, that's terrific. I'll go up to my room first and will be right back. Thank you very much.

Rezeptionist/-in: 16. ______________________________

____

____

Dealing with Guests in the Hotel

149

Bitte finden Sie je zwei englischsprachige Umsetzungen zu jeder der unten stehenden Situationen.

Die Rezeptionistin/der Rezeptionist ...

1. ... fragt den Gast, ob er reserviert hat.
2. ... teilt mit, dass keine Zimmer mehr frei sind.
3. ... bittet den Gast um das Ausfüllen des Anmeldeformulars.
4. ... händigt die Schlüssel aus.
5. ... führt den Gast zu seinem Zimmer.
6. ... nennt die Zimmernummer.
7. ... empfiehlt etwas (z. B. die Benutzung des ÖPNV).
8. ... rät von etwas ab (z. B. von der Benutzung des ÖPNV).
9. ... fragt nach besonderen Wünschen.
10. ... bedauert einen Wunsch ablehnen zu müssen.
11. ... erkundigt sich, ob alles in Ordnung ist.
12. ... erwidert Dank des Gastes.
13. ... fragt nach, weil sie/er etwas nicht verstanden hat.

150

Vergleichen Sie nun bitte Ihre Lösungen in Ihrer Arbeitsgruppe und vervollständigen Sie Ihre Listen.

151

Entwerfen Sie bitte für die unten skizzierte Situation einen englischen Dialog. Dieser Dialog sollte alle Situationen umfassen, die sich von dem Moment an ergeben, wenn ein Gast das Hotel betritt, bis hin zur Schlüsselübergabe.

Ein Englisch sprechender Gast betritt das Hotel um 20:15 Uhr und möchte sein reserviertes Zimmer beziehen.

Er bekommt die üblichen Fragen (Name, Nationalität, Zahlungsart usw.) gestellt.

Er erkundigt sich, ob das Zimmer zum Park hin gelegen ist.

Dies ist nicht der Fall.

Er hätte jedoch gerne ein solches Zimmer.

Ihm wird eins angeboten, das allerdings € 42,00 teurer ist.

Er akzeptiert; und fragt, ob es möglich ist, das Frühstück auf dem Zimmer serviert zu bekommen.

Dies wird bestätigt, mit dem Hinweis, dass er den Zimmerservice jederzeit über Nr. 22 anrufen kann, um Bestellungen aufzugeben.

4268168

152

Setzen Sie bitte die folgenden Sprechabsichten in einen englischen Dialog um.

Words and phrases you might find helpful:

bank transfer	dry-cleaning	item
cash	embarassing	regular
check	to freeze	unfortunate

Mrs Gibson, der Stammgast mit den höchsten Trinkgeldern, kommt vor dem Frühstück an die Rezeption.

Gast:	1.	erinnert daran, dass sie heute abreisen will; fragt, ob Rechnung fertig ist.
Rezeptionst/-in:	2.	bestätigt, händigt die Rechnung aus und fragt, ob wie üblich mit Kreditkarte gezahlt werden soll.
Gast:	3.	bejaht, kontrolliert die Rechnung und bestätigt, dass sie drei kleine Flaschen Gin und fünf Mal Bitterlemon aus der Minibar gehabt hat; ist erstaunt über den Preis und fragt in scherzendem Ton, ob das überhaupt legal sei.
Rezeptionst/-in:	4.	geht auf den scherzenden Ton ein: eigentlich nicht, aber so kann man etwas Geld nebenher verdienen.
Gast:	5.	lobt die Eigeninitiative; kann ihre Kreditkarte nicht finden und muss zurück aufs Zimmer, um sie zu holen.
Rezeptionst/-in:	6.	?
		Nach einigen Minuten:
Gast:	7.	ist verzweifelt, da Kreditkarte nicht zu finden; glaubt sie verloren zu haben.
Rezeptionst/-in:	8.	bedauert; bietet an die Gesellschaft anzurufen, um die Karte sperren zu lassen.
Gast:	9.	bedankt sich dafür; weiß aber nicht, wie sie zahlen soll, da sie nur eine *Bust-Finance-Card* zur Hand hat.
Rezeptionst/-in:	10.	werden leider nicht akzeptiert; vielleicht Reiseschecks?
Gast:	11.	hat keine und auch nicht genug Bargeld.
Rezeptionst/-in:	12.	beruhigt; bietet für sie als Stammkundin die Möglichkeit an, nach ihrer Rückkehr vom Heimatort aus per Banküberweisung zu zahlen.
Gast:	13.	ist etwas skeptisch.
Rezeptionst/-in:	14.	kein Problem.
Gast:	15.	ist erleichtert.
Rezeptionst/-in:	16.	nicht der Rede wert; wird jetzt die Kreditkartengesellschaft anrufen.
Gast:	17.	sehr freundlich.
Rezeptionst/-in:	18.	keine Ursache.
		Nach dem Frühstück:
Gast:	19.	hat noch eine Frage zur Rechnung.
Rezeptionst/-in:	20.	?
Gast:	21.	betont, dass sie sich nicht beschweren will: zeigt ein bestimmtes Wort auf der Rechnung, das sie nicht versteht.
Rezeptionst/-in:	22.	erinnert daran, dass ein Mantel zur chemischen Reinigung geschickt wurde.
Gast:	23.	erinnert sich; bedankt sich für die Auskunft.
Rezeptionst/-in:	24.	gern geschehen.

Complaints and Special Wishes in the Hotel

153

Ordnen Sie bitte die Nummern aus den Bildern M33/M34 den jeweiligen Begriffen zu und finden Sie die deutschen Ausdrücke.

Living Room/Bedroom	Nr.	Wohn-/Schlafraum
air conditioning		
alarm clock		
ashtray		
bed table		
carpet		
coat hanger		
coffee table		
curtain		
cushion		
desk		
double bed		
dressing table		
fireplace		
heating		
lamp		
mattress		
minibar		
mirror		
pillow		
quilt		
radiator		
reading lamp		
rug		
sheet		
single bed		
sofa/settee		
telephone		
thermostat		
trouser press		
TV/television		
twin bed		
wardrobe		
wastepaper basket		

Bathroom	Nr.	Badezimmer
cistern		
comb		
faucet/(BE) tap		
flannel		
garbage bin		
mirror		
plug		
(electric) razor		
razorblade		
shampoo		
shower		
soap		
socket		
sponge		
toilet		
toilet roll/paper		
toilet seat		
toothbrush		
toothpaste		
towel		
washbasin		

Complaints and Special Wishes in the Hotel

Ein Gast ruft an der Rezeption mit einer Beschwerde an.

Gast:	Excuse me, miss, but the bed in my room has not been made.
Rezeptionistin:	Oh I'm really sorry, madam, I'll send someone up to make it at once.

154

Formulieren Sie jetzt bitte einige Beschwerden über fehlende, beschädigte usw. Dinge aus der Liste auf S. 170 und die angemessenen Reaktionen darauf.

Words and phrases you might find helpful:

Complaints	**Reactions**	
broken/dirty/torn	to apologize	to ask/to send someone immediately
doesn't work	very/really	to change/to replace
missing	I'll see to it at once.	to clean/to empty

Bei der Ankunft äußert ein Gast an der Rezeption eine spezielle Bitte.

Gast:	I'm afraid I've forgotten to bring my soap! Could you get me some, please?
Rezeptionist/-in:	Certainly, miss, no problem. There already is a small cake in your bathroom, but I'll send you some extra ones.
Gast:	That'd be very kind. Thank you very much indeed.
Rezeptionist/-in:	You're welcome, miss.

155

Formulieren Sie nun bitte einige Sonderwünsche, die ein Gast haben könnte, sowie die angemessenen Reaktionen darauf. Die unten vorgegebene Liste soll Ihnen eine Anregung geben.

Words and phrases you might find helpful:

florist's	telephone directory
launderette	I'm afraid that's not possible, (sir/madam/miss,) because ...

- A stain on a blouse/shirt/skirt
- Theater tickets for tomorrow night
- Flowers for a businessfriend's wife
- An extra armchair for her/his room
- Telephone number of a certain person
- Departure time of plane/train

„Ihr" Hotel hat eine Anfrage erhalten (→ M36). Sie werden gebeten diesen Brief mit einem deutschsprachigen Memo der Salesmanagerin zur Bearbeitung vorzulegen.

156 Schreiben Sie bitte die zur Bearbeitung der Anfrage benötigten Informationen heraus.

Memo

____

____

____

____

____

____

____

____

____

____

____

____

____

____

Auf der Grundlage Ihres Memos hat die Salesmanagerin, Meta Mustermann, ihrem Mitarbeiter Ole Olsen die Anfrage sowie die nachfolgend wiedergegebene Notiz auf den Schreibtisch gelegt.

- *Bitte Schreiben der Leatherstocking Inc. beantworten*
- *Übliche Antwort mit Hotelprospekt u. Preisliste*
- *Zusätzlich auf folgende Punkte hinweisen:*
  a) Preisnachlass von 15 % für Konferenzen mit mind. 50 Teilnehmern
  b) Angebot: 3 Mahlzeiten pro Tag für € 155,00 pro Person
  c) Möglichkeit zur Teilnahme am Musikfestival u. Galadiner

Mustermann

Das Ergebnis ist das Angebotsschreiben M37.

4268172

157

Ergänzen Sie gegebenenfalls diese Auflistung.

Some alternative phrases

a) we thank you for your letter dated August 16 concerning	• thank you very much for your letter dated • we thank you for your letter of 16 August in which you • we were pleased to receive your letter • ___ • ___
b) we are looking forward to hearing from you soon	• please answer as soon as possible • this offer is valid only until • we would appreciate your rapid reply • ___ • ___
c) we would like to submit the following offer	• we can make an offer under the following terms and conditions • ___ • ___
d) ___	• ___ • ___

Correspondence: Offer

Ihr Hotel hat ein Schreiben mit der folgenden Anfrage erhalten.

From 2nd till 14th November we would like to book rooms for fifteen members of our firm. In addition we will need a conference room for the whole time and for the last two days we would like to arrange an exhibition of our products for the German partners of our firm (a room of about 250 m^2 will be needed for that); enclosed please find for your information a brochure which shows a variety of our products.

As eight of us will be accompanied by wives or husbands, we would appreciate it if you could help organizing a program for their entertainment for some of the days during the time of our stay.

Please send us information about the prices of your meals, as we would like to take them individually according to our needs and likings.

158

Verfassen Sie unter Ihrem Namen ein Angebot – einen formal vollständigen Geschäftsbrief mit heutigem Datum – auf der Grundlage der folgenden Stichwörter als Antwort auf die oben stehende Anfrage. Bringen Sie die einzelnen Punkte in eine sinnvolle Reihenfolge.

Words and phrases you might find helpful:

p.d. = per day	to allow/to grant a reduction	facilities
p.n. = per night	at a total of	latest technical equipment
p.p. = per person	equipped with	

Da für die infrage kommende Zeit Sonderaktionen geplant sind, können Sie der anfragenden Firma nicht wie üblich Hotelbroschüren schicken, sondern müssen die Einzelposten im Brief nennen.

Einzelzimmer: € 115,00 pro Nacht

Adresse: Renaissance, Ltd.
1 The Mall
London SW1
Great Britain

Ihre Sekretärin heißt: Marthe Schwerdtlein

Mittagessen: € 16,50 bis € 35,00

Programm für Ehepartner kann organisiert werden (Ausflüge, Besichtigungen, Einkaufsbummel u. Ä.)

Der Sekretär des Adressaten heißt: Ben Jonson

Kein Preisnachlass möglich

Konferenzraum für 15 Personen (modernste technische Ausstattung): € 210,00 pro Tag (reduzierter Sonderpreis!)

Frühstücksbüfett: € 13,00

Zweitägige Ausstellung der Produkte kann arrangiert werden; zwei miteinander verbundene Räume à 120 m^2 zu insgesamt € 500,00 pro Tag

Mittag- u. Abendessen: à la carte

Absender:
Haus zur Bruchbude
Sumpfgasse 123
45678 Kleinkleckersdorf

Abendessen: ab € 16,00

Verfasser der Anfrage ist:
Christopher Marlowe
Senior Executive Manager
Renaissance, Ltd.

Doppelzimmer: € 80,00 pro Person und Nacht

4268174

159

Ergänzen Sie gegebenenfalls diese Auflistung.

Some alternative phrases

a) which we hereby confirm

- herewith we confirm
- this is to confirm
-
-

b) we look forward to welcoming you in

- we're expecting you by August 3
- your rooms will be ready
-
-

c) any further wishes will find our careful attention

- please let us know if
- should any further wishes arise, please do not hesitate to contact us
-
-

d)

-
-

Correspondence: Reminder

160

Ergänzen Sie gegebenenfalls diese Auflistung.

Some alternative phrases

a) may we draw your attention to the fact that

- may we remind you of our invoice
- as you have not yet settled our invoice we would like to
-
-

b) please see to this matter

- please settle the matter
- please make sure that
-
-

c) in the near future

- within the next few days
- by the end of August
-
-

Second reminder

d) as you disregarded our letter of May 27

-

e) if you should also disregard this reminder we shall be forced to take legal action against you

-

Das Hotel „Haus zur Bruchbude" hat eine Anfrage erhalten (→ M41), der leider nicht entsprochen werden kann. Um jedoch einen möglicherweise guten Kunden nicht zu verlieren macht das Salesoffice einen Gegenvorschlag (→ M42).

161

Ergänzen Sie gegebenenfalls diese Auflistung.

Some alternative phrases

a) as we are fully booked

- due to the fact that we are
- being outbooked we are not able to
- ______________________________
- ______________________________

b) we regret that we have to inform you

- we are sorry to say that
- ______________________________
- ______________________________

c) we are in no position to carry out

- we are unable to execute
- ______________________________
- ______________________________

d) we trust that our situation finds your kind understanding

- that this difficulty will not overshadow our good business relations
- we most sincerely hope that
- ______________________________
- ______________________________

e) ______________________________

- ______________________________

Application

162

Schreiben Sie bitte zunächst Ihren Lebenslauf (komplett mit allen Daten und Fakten).

Curriculum Vitae

Name

Address

Telephone/Telefax

Date of Birth

Place of Birth

Nationality

Education

Qualifications

163

Verfassen Sie dann zur Übung zwei Bewerbungen:

- eine als direkte Antwort auf eine Anzeige,
- eine als „kalte Bewerbung", d. h. eine Bewerbung, ohne dass ein spezifisches Angebot vorliegt.

Nehmen Sie ein Hotel Ihrer Wahl oder greifen Sie auf die Betriebe zurück, die Sie in M49 erwähnt finden.

4268178

Abbreviations – Abkürzungen

CV	(lateinisch: Curriculum Vitae)	Curriculum Vitae	Lebenslauf
e.g.	(lateinisch: exempli gratia)	for example, for instance	zum Beispiel
esp.		especially	besonders (z. B.)
etc.	(lateinisch: et cetera)	et cetera	und so weiter
i.e.	(lateinisch: id est)	that is	das ist (d. i.)
p.d.		per day	pro Tag
p.n.		per night	pro Nacht
p.p.		per person	pro Person
viz.	(lateinisch: videlicet)	videlicet	nämlich

Bildquellenverzeichnis:

CMA, Bonn	10 (1, 3, 4)
CMA, Bonn/ABC Euro RSCG	7, 8 (1)
„Deutsche See" GmbH & Co. KG, Bremerhaven	9
Dorint AG, Mönchengladbach	83
Gesellschaft für Öffentlichkeitsarbeit der Deutschen Brauwirtschaft e.V., Bonn	110
Hefele Fotodesign, Darmstadt	5, 6 (oben), 8 (2, 3), 10 (2, 5), 11 (1, 2), 12, 13, 24, 55
Hild, Claudia	27, 28
Kaip, Boris	25, 29
Oryza, Hamburg	11 (3)
SALOMON HITBURGER GmbH, Großostheim-Ringheim	6 (unten)
Schmitz, Ansgar/Mosel-Saar-Ruwer Wein e.V., Trier	150

(BE) Nur im britischen Englisch gebräuchlich.

(MZ) Dieses Wort wird nur in der Mehrzahl gebraucht.

A

Aal eel
Abart variety
abbiegen to turn
abbrühen (blanchieren) to blanch
Abfahrt departure
Abfalleimer garbage bin
Abflug departure
Abgang finish
abgestanden stale
abgestimmt matched
Ablehnung refusal
abreisen to leave
Absage refusal
abseihen to strain
Abseiher strainer
Absender sender's name
Ahornsirup maple sirup
akzeptieren, annehmen to accept
Alkohol alcohol
alkoholfrei non-alcoholic, alcohol free
Alkoholgehalt (hoher/niedriger ~) alcohol contents (high/low ~)
alkoholhaltig alcoholic
alkoholisch alcoholic
Allee avenue
Allerheiligen All Saints' Day
alt old
altmodisch old fashioned
Amerika America
Amerikaner/-in American
amerikanisch American
amerikanische Heidelbeere(n) huckleberry/-ies
Ananas pineapple
an der Ecke on the corner
Anfrage enquiry, inquiry
Angebot offer
angebrannt burnt
angleichen to assimilate
anglikanisch Anglican
Angriff attack
Anis (Pflanze) anise / (Samen) aniseed
Anklang touch
Ankunft arrival
Anlage (zu einem Brief) Enc., Encs. (enclosure)
anmachen (z. B. Salat) to toss, (besonders BE) to dress
annehmen, akzeptieren to accept
Anrede (in einem Brief) salutation
Anzahl number
Apfel apple
Apfelsine orange
Appetitanreger appetizer
Aprikose apricot
April April
aromatisieren to flavor, (BE) to flavour
aromatisieren (mit Spirituosen) to lace
Art variety
Artischocke artichoke
Aschenbecher ashtray
Asiate/Asiatin Asian
asiatisch Asian
Asien Asia
assimilieren to assimilate
Aubergine aubergine, (BE) egg plant
aufgespriteter Wein fortified wine
aufmerksam attentive
Aufschnitt cold cuts, sausage slices
Aufzug elevator, (BE) lift
August August
ausbacken (frittieren) to deep fry
ausdrücken to squeeze
ausdrücklich (Adjektiv) explicit, (Adverb) explicitly
ausgebucht fully booked
ausgedehnt extensive
ausgestattet mit equipped with
ausgewogen balanced
Ausgewogenheit balance
ausgleichen to counterbalance
ausleeren to empty
Aussicht haben/bieten to overlook
Ausstattung (technisch) equipment
Ausstellungsgelände exposition ground, fair ground
Auswahl selection, choice
auswechseln to change, to replace

B

backen to bake
Backpflaume prune
Badezimmer bathroom
Bahnhof station
Balance balance
Banane banana
Bank (Geldinstitut) bank
Bank (Sitzmöbel) bench
Banknote bill, (BE) note
Banküberweisung bank transfer
bar cash
Bar bar
Barlöffel bar spoon
Barsieb strainer
Barspieß stick
Basilikum basil
beauftragen to ask
Becher (große Tasse) mug
Bedienung service
Bedienungsgeld service charge
Beere(n) berry/-ies
behaglich cozy, (BE) cosy
Beifuß mugwort
Beilage side dish, side order
Beistelltisch coffee table
bekömmlich wholesome
beliebt popular
bequem comfortable, cozy, (BE) cosy
berechnen to charge
bewerben (sich bewerben um) to apply
Bewerbung application
Bierwärmer beer warmer
Birne pear
bitten to ask
bitter bitter
blanchieren to blanch
Blätterteig puff pastry
blau (Steak) raw
Blaubeere(n) blueberry/-ies
Blick haben/bieten to overlook
Blumenhandlung florist's
Blumenkohl cauliflower
blumig flowery
Bluse blouse
Blut blood
blutig (Steak) raw
Blutwurst black pudding
Böhme/Böhmin Bohemian
Böhmen Bohemia
böhmisch Bohemian
Bohne bean
Bohnenkraut (summer) savory
Bordeaux(wein) (rot) claret
Bouillion broth
braten (kurz) to fry
braten (lang) to roast
Bratkartoffeln fried potatoes
Bratkartoffeln (aus Streifen von rohen Kartoffeln) (AE) hash browns
Bratwurst sausage
Brauerei brewery
Brieftext body of the letter
Briefverkehr correspondence
Bries sweetbreads
Brite/Britin Briton
Brokkoli broccoli
Brombeere(n) blackberry/-ies
Brot bread
Brotkorb bread basket
Brotmesser (zum Streichen) side knife
Brotteller side plate
Brücke (Teppich) rug
Brunnenkresse watercress
Brust breast
buchen to book, to order, to reserve
Buchung booking, order, reservation
Büfett buffet
Burg castle
Burgunder(wein) Burgundy
Büro office
Busfahrt bus ride
Buß- und Bettag Day of Repentance

4268180

Butterbrot sandwich, open sandwich
Buttermesser butter knife
Butterschälchen butter dish

C

Cayennepfeffer Cayenne, Cayenne pepper
Champagner champagne
Champignon champignon, mushroom
chemische Reinigung dry-cleaning
Chili chile, (BE) chilli
China China
Chinakohl Chinese cabbage
Chinese/Chinesin Chinese
chinesisch Chinese
Christi Himmelfahrt Ascension Day
Chutney (ein würziges Mus aus klein geschnittenen Früchten und/oder Gemüsen mit Essig, Gewürzen und Kräutern) chutney
Cocktailglas cocktail glass
Cocktailstick cocktail stick
Consommé strong broth, consommé
Cornflakes cornflakes
Couch couch, settee, sofa
Court-bouillon fish broth
Couvert cover
Crasheis crushed ice
Creme cream
Croissant croissant
Curry (Gewürzmischung) curry

D

dämpfen to steam
Damwild (Tier) fallow deer
Däne/Dänin Dane
Dänemark Denmark
dänisch Danish
Darbietung presentation
darren to kiln-dry
Dattel date
Datum date
deftig good and solid, traditional
dekantieren decant
Dekantierkorb wine basket
Dekoration decoration
dekorativ decorative
dekorieren to decorate
denkmalgeschütztes Gebäude listed building
Dessert dessert
Dezember December
Diabetes diabetes
Diabetiker diabetic
Diät diet
dick thick
dicke Bohne broad bean
Dienstleistung service
Dill dill
Dom cathedral
dominieren to dominate
Doppelbett double bed
dunkel dark
dünsten to stew
Durchreiche serving hatch
durchsieben to sieve
Dusche shower

E

Eckbank corner seat
Ecke corner
ehrlich gesagt frankly
Ei egg
Eierbecher egg-cup
Eiklar egg white
eindicken to thicken
einfüllen to fill
einhüllen to wrap, to encase
Einkaufspassage shopping gallery, shopping mall
Einkaufszone shopping area
einlegen to pickle
Einrichtung (technisch) equipment
Einrichtung, Hoteleinrichtung facility
einschließen (einbeziehen) to include
Einzelbett single bed
Einzelbetten (zwei ~) twin beds
Eis(creme) ice cream
Eisbox icecube box
Eiswürfel ice cube
Eiszange ice-tongs
Elch (amerikanischer ~) moose, (europäischer ~) elk
elegant elegant, stylish
elektrisch electric
Empfangsdame, -herr receptionist
empfehlen to recommend
Empfehlung recommendation
Empfindung sensation
Endivie endive
englisch (Steak) rare
englische Creme custard
Ente duck
entkoffeiniert decaffeinated
entlang along
Erbse pea
Erdbeere(n) strawberry/-ies
Erdnuss peanut
erfrischend refreshing
erleichtern to ease someone's mind
Ernährung diet, food
Ernährungsvorschriften dietary rules
Ersatz substitute
ersetzen to replace
erstaunlich astonishing
Erster Mai (Tag der Arbeit) May Bank Holiday
erster Weihnachtstag Christmas Day
Essen (Art der Speisenzubereitung) cooking, cuisine, food
Essen (Mahlzeit) meal
Essenz (concentrated soup served in small quantities) essence
Essig vinegar
Esskastanie chestnut
Esslöffel tablespoon
Estragon tarragon
Etikett label
Eule owl
Europa Europe
Europäer/-in European
europäisch European
evangelisch Protestant

F

Fabrik plant, factory
Fachwerk(haus) half timbered (house)
fad dull
Fahrplan timetable
Falke hawk
Farbe coloring, (BE) colouring
Farbstoff coloring, (BE) colouring
Fasan pheasant
fasten to fast
Fastenzeit Lent
Februar February
fehlen to miss
Fehler fault
Feige fig
fein fine
Feldsalat lamb's lettuce
Fenchel fennel
fermentieren to ferment
Fernseher television, TV
Fernsehgerät television, TV
Fett fat
fettfrei fat-free
Fettgehalt (hier: mit niedrigem ~) low-fat
Filet fillet
filetieren to fillet
filieren to fillet
filtern to filter
finnisch Finnish
Finnland Finland
Fisch fish / three fish (Anzahl), three fishes (Arten)
Fischgang fish course
Fitnessraum multigym
flach flat
flambieren to flambé
flambiert flambé, flambéed
Flaschenöffner bottle opener
Fleisch meat
Fleischteile pieces of meat
Flosse fin
Flughafen airport
Flugplan timetable
Flugzeug plane
Flüssigkeit liquid
Folienkartoffel baked (jacket) potato
Forelle trout
Form mold, (BE) mould
fragen to ask
Frankreich France
Franzose/Französin Frenchman/Frenchwoman
französisch French
Frau (in einer Anrede, z. B. Brief) Mrs
Fräulein (in einer Anrede, z. B. Brief) Miss

freundlich friendly
Friedhof cemetery
friedlich peaceful, restful
frisch fresh
frittieren to deep-fry
Fronleichnam Feast of Corpus Christi
Früchtemesser fruit knife
fruchtig fruity
Fruchtpresse fruit press
Frühstückstasse breakfast cup
füllen to fill
füllen, stopfen to stuff
Fußgängerüberweg pedestrians' crossing
Fußgängerzone pedestrians' area

G

Gang course
Gans/Gänse goose/geese
Garderobe cloakroom, wardrobe
Gardine curtain, drape
garen to cook
gären to ferment
Garnele shrimp
garnieren to garnish
Gärung fermentation
Garverfahren ways of cooking
gar ziehen (pochieren) to poach
Gasse alley
Gaumen palate
Gebäude building
Gebiet area
Gedeck(preis) cover charge
Geflügel poultry
gegart cooked
Geier vulture
gekocht cooked
gekochtes Ei boiled egg
Geldschein bill, (BE) note
Geldüberweisung (ohne Ansehen der Methode) remittance
Gelee jelly
Gemüse vegetable
Gemüsesaft vegetable juice
gemütlich cozy, (BE) cosy
Gepäck baggage
Gepäckträger porter
geradeaus straight on
Gerbsäure tannin
Gericht dish, meal
Gerste barley
Gesamtbild general impression
Geschäft business
geschäftig busy
Geschäftsfreund businessfriend
Geschäftsführer manager
Geschirr crockery, plates and dishes
geschmacklos tasteless
gestoßenes Eis crushed ice
gesund (zur Beschreibung von Lebensmitteln) good for you
Gesundheit health
Getreide corn, grain
Getreideprodukte cereal
Gewürz spice
Gewürzgurke pickle, (BE) gherkin
gewürzt spicy
gießen to pour
glänzend bright
Gläser glassware
glasieren to glaze
Golfplatz golf course
Gottesdienst service
Grapefruit grapefruit
gratinieren to gratinate
gratiniert gratinated, au gratin
Grieche/Griechin Greek
Griechenland Greece
griechisch Greek
grillen (nur Fleisch) to barbecue
grillen to broil, (BE) to grill
groß (hier: hoch gewachsen) tall
groß big
großartig great, marvellous
Großbritannien Great Britain
Großstadt city
grundsätzlich basic
grüne Bohne French bean
Grünkohl (curly/green) kale
grünlich (bläulich, -lich) greenish (blueish, -ish)
Gurke cucumber
gut good, fine
gut durch well done
gut gewürzt well seasoned

H

Hachse knuckle
hacken to chop
Hafer oats
Haferbrei porridge
Haferflocken oatmeal
Halbinsel peninsula
Hälfte half (one/a half of ...)
Haltestelle stop
Hammel(fleisch) mutton
Handdusche shower
Handtuch towel
hart hard, solid
Hase hare
Haselnuss hazelnut
Hauptbahnhof central station
Hauptgang main course
Hauptnahrung(smittel) staple diet
hauptsächlich main, major
Haus house (als Gebäude nur für Ein-/Zweifamilienhäuser bzw. Reihenhäuser)
Haxe knuckle
Hecht pike
Hefe yeast
Heidelbeere(n) blueberry/-ies, (amerik. ~) huckleberry/-ies
Heilbutt halibut
Heiligabend Christmas Eve
heiß hot
Heizkörper radiator
Heizung heating
hell (Bier) pale / (Wein) light
Hemd shirt
Hemmung inhibition
herb dry
Hering herring
Herr (in einer Anrede, z. B. Brief) Mr
Herz heart
herzhaft hearty
Himbeere(n) raspberry/-ies
hindurchgeben (durch Sieb, Strainer ...) to pass through (a sieve, a strainer...)
hinter behind
hinzufügen to add
Hirn brain
hochflitzen (salopp) to pop up
höflich courteous, polite
holländisch Dutch
Holzbalken wooden beam
Holzvertäfelung wood panelling
Honigmelone honeydew melon
Hopfen (Pflanze) hop / (getrocknet, als Brauzutat) hops
hopfenbetont (salopp) hoppy
Hotel-/Gaststättengewerbe hotel and catering business
Hoteleinrichtung(en) facility/-ies
Huhn chicken
Hummer lobster

I

Iberische Halbinsel Iberian Peninsula
Inder/-in Indian
Indianer/-in Indian
indianisch Indian
Indien India
indisch Indian
Indonesien Indonesia
Indonesier/-in Indonesian
indonesisch Indonesian
Ingwer ginger
Inneneinrichtung interior
Innenstadt center, (BE) centre
Innereien offal
Insel island
international international
Irland Ireland, Eire (gälischer Name Irlands)
Islam Islam
islamisch Islamic
Italien Italy
italienisch Italian
Jahr year
Jahrgang vintage
Jakobsmuschel scallop
Januar January
Japan Japan
Japaner/-in Japanese
japanisch Japanese
Jasmin jasmin
Johannisbeere black currant, red currant
Jude, Jüdin Jew
Judentum Judaism
jüdisch Jewish

4268182

Vokabular: Deutsch – Englisch

Juli July
jung (Gemüse) young
Juni June

K

Kabeljau cod
Kachelofen tiled stove
Kaffee coffee
Kaffeekanne coffee pot
Kaiserschoten sugar peas
Kalb (Tier) calf
Kalb(fleisch) veal
Kalorie(n) calory/-ies
kalorienarm low-in-calories
kalorienreich rich-in-calories
kalt cold
Kamin fireplace
Kamm comb
Kaninchen rabbit
Karaffe carafe, decanter
Karamell caramel
Karfreitag Good Friday
Karpfen carp
Karte (z. B. Eintritts~, Fahr~ ...) ticket
Kartoffel(n) potato(es)
Kartoffelbrei mashed potatoes
Kartoffelkroketten potato croquettes, croquette potatoes
Kartoffelpüree mashed potatoes
Käse cheese
Kasse cash register
Kassenbeleg receipt
Kassenbon receipt
Kastanie chestnut
Kaste (religiöse und soziale Schicht) caste
katholisch catholic
Kaviar caviar
keimen to germinate
Kellner/-in waiter
Kellnermesser waiter's friend
Kerbel chervil
Keule leg
Kino cinema
Kirche church
Kirsche(n) cherry/-ies
klar clear
klare Brühe broth, bouillon
Kleiderbügel coat hanger
Kleiderschrank wardrobe
Kleiderständer coat stand
Klimaanlage air conditioning (mit Klimaanlage: air conditioned)
Kloß dumpling
knackig crispy
Knoblauch garlic
Knödel dumpling
knusprig crunchy
Koch (allgemein) cook
Koch (professionell, im Restaurant) chef
Kochen (Art der Speisenzubereitung) cooking
kochen (bei 100 °C in Wasser garen) to boil
kochen (im Sinne von garen) to cook
Kohl cabbage
Kohlrabi kohlrabi
Kokosnuss coconut
Kombination combination
Konfitüre jam, fruit preserve
Konserve (hier: Marmelade, Gelee usw.) preserve
konservieren to preserve
Konservierungsmittel preservative
konsumieren to consume
Kopfkissen pillow
Kopfschmerzen headache
Korken cork
Korkenzieher corkscrew
Körper body
körperreich fullbodied
Kotelett cutlet
Kraftbrühe strong broth, consommé
Krake octupus
Kräuter herbs
Krebs crayfish
Kreditkarte credit card
Krem cream
Krone (Bier) head
krönen to crown
Krusten- und Schaltiere shellfish
Küche (Art der Speisenzubereitung) cooking, cuisine, food
Küche (Ort) kitchen
Kuchen cake
kulinarisch culinary
Kultur culture
Kümmel (Pflanze) caraway / (Samen) carawayseed
Kupfer copper
Kürbis pumpkin

L

Lachs salmon
Lage location
Lamm (Tier) lamb
Lamm(fleisch) lamb
Lampe lamp
Land country
Languste crawfish
lästig fallen to make a nuisance of (oneself/herself ...)
Lateinamerika Latin America
Lauch leek
Läufer (Teppich) rug
lauwarm lukewarm
Lebenslauf Curriculum Vitae, CV
Lebensmittel food
Leber liver
lecker tasty
legal legal
leicht light
Leselampe reading lamp
liegen (hier: örtliche Platzierung) to be located, to be situated
Likör liqueur
Limone lime
links left
Linse (Hülsenfrucht) lentil
Liter liter, (BE) litre
Löffel spoon
Löffelbiskuit finger biscuit
lokal local
Longdrinkglas longdrink glass
Lorbeerblatt/-blätter bay leaf/leaves
Lunge (hier: kulinarisch) (MZ) lights
Lunge (Organ) lung(s)

M

Magen stomach
mager lean, low-fat, low in fat
Mahl meal
Mahlzeit meal
Mahnung reminder
Mai May
Mais corn, (BE) maize
Maische mash
maischen to mash
Majoran marjoram
Makrele mackerel
Malz malt
malzig malty
Mandel almond
Mangold (Swiss) chard
marinieren to marinade, to marinate
Mark marrow
Marmelade jam, fruit preserve
Marmeladentöpfchen preserve dish
Marone chestnut
März March
Maß measure
Maßeinheit measure
Matratze mattress
Medaillon medallion
medium (Steak) medium
Meerrettich horseradish
Mehl flour
Mehrwertsteuer VAT (Value Added Tax)
Melone melon
Menage (als Zutat) condiment (als Gegenstand) cruet (stand)
Messbecher jigger
Messe (Ausstellung) exhibition, exposition, fair
Messe (Gelände) exposition ground, fair ground
Messe (Religion) mass
Mexikaner/-in Mexican
mexikanisch Mexican
Mexiko Mexico
Miesmuschel mussel
Milch milk
Milch, fettarm skim milk
Milchkännchen milk jug
mild mild
Minibar minibar
Minze mint
mischen to mix
Mittagessen lunch, (sprachlich korrekte, wenn auch kaum noch gebräuchliche Form) luncheon
Mitteleuropa Central Europe

Mittelmeer Mediterranean Sea
Mittelmeerländer Mediterranean Countries
Mixbecher shaker
mixen to mix
Mixer blender, Hamilton, mixer
Mixglas mixing glass
möbliert furnished
Möblierung furnishing
Mode fashion
modern modern
Möglichkeiten, Hoteleinrichtungen facilities
Mohn (Pflanze) poppy / (Samen) poppy seed
Möhre carrot
Mokka mocha
Monat month
Morchel morel
Mosel (Fluss u. Wein) Moselle
Most must
Museum museum
Muskatnuss nutmeg
Müsli granola

N

nach after
Nachbarschaft neighborhood, (BE) neighbourhood
Nachspeise dessert
Nachttisch bed table
nah near
nahe (bei) close (to)
Nahverkehr public transport
Nase (= Geruch) nose
neben next to
nebenbei on the side
nebenher on the side
Nelke (Blume) carnation
Nelke (Gewürz) clove
Nelkenpfeffer pimento
Neujahr New Year's Day
nicht gar not done
Nichtraucherzone no-smoking area
Niere kidney
Niveau level
Norwegen Norway
Norweger/-in Norwegian
norwegisch Norwegian
November November
Nudeln pasta
Nussnugataufstrich chocolate spread

O

obergärig top-fermented beer/top fermenting yeast
Obst fruit
Ochse (Tier) ox
Ochsenfleisch beef
offen gesagt frankly
Öffnungszeiten opening hours
Oktober October
Öl oil
ölig (Wein: dick) thick
Olive olive
Omelett omelette
Oper opera
ÖPNV (öffentl. Personennahverk.) local public transportation system, (BE) local public transport system
Orangenmarmelade (bitter, mit Schalenstücken) marmalade
Orangensaft orange juice
Oregano oregano
örtlich local
Ostasien East-Asia
Ostern Easter

P

Pampelmuse grapefruit
paniert breaded, coated with bread crumbs
Papierkorb wastepaper basket
Paprika (sweet) pepper
Park park
Parkanlagen park grounds
Parkhaus multi storey car park
Parkplatz parking lot, (BE) car park
Paste paste
Pastete pie
Pastinake parsnip
Pazifischer Ozean Pacific Ocean
peinlich embarrassing
Pellkartoffeln (boiled) jacket potatoes
Periode (geschichtlicher Zeitabschnitt) period
Perlhuhn guinea fowl
Petersilie parsley
Pfannkuchen pancake
Pfeffer pepper
Pfifferling chanterelle
Pfingsten Whitsun
Pfirsich(e) peach/-es
Pflaume plum
Pförtner doorman
Philippine, Philippinin Filipino, Philippine
Philippinen Philippines
philippinisch Filipino, Philippine
pikant spicy
Pilz mushroom
Piment pimento
Pistazie pistachio
Platz (z. B. im Restaurant) seat
pochieren to poach
pochiertes Ei poached egg
pökeln to corn
Pole/Polin Pole
Polen Poland
polnisch Polish
Pommes frites French fries, (BE) chips
populär popular
Porree leek
Portugal Portugal
Portugiese/Portugiesin Portuguese
portugiesisch Portuguese
Portwein port
Posten (auf einer Rechnung) item
Poularde chicken
Präsentation presentation
Preis (Geld) price
Preis (Gewinn) prize
protestantisch Protestant
Prozent percent, per cent
Pudding pudding (auch im Englischen inzwischen als Synonym für *Flammeri* gebraucht)
Punkt (auf einer Rechnung) item
pürieren to mash
Puter turkey

Q

Quark curd
Quitte quince

R

Radieschen radish/-es
Ragout ragout, stew
Rasierer razor
Rasierklinge razorblade
rau rough
räuchern to smoke
Rebhuhn partridge
Rechnung bill (nur im amerikanischen Englisch benutzt: check)
rechtens legal
rechts right
reetgedeckt thatched
Regal shelf
regelmäßig regular
regional regional
Rehwild (Tier) roe deer
reif ripe, mature
Reifung maturation
Reihenfolge order, sequence
Reinigung (MZ) cleaners
Reis rice
reservieren to book, to order, to reserve
Reservierung reservation, booking
Restaurant restaurant
Rezept recipe
Rhabarber rhubarb
Rheinwein Rhine wine, (eher umgangssprachlich: hock)
Rind (Tier) cow
Rind(fleisch) beef
Rock skirt
Rogen roe
Roggen rye
roh raw
Rosé rosé
Rosenkohl Brussels sprouts
Rosenmontag Carnival Monday
Rosine raisin
Rosmarin rosemary
Rote Bete beetroot
rote Johannisbeere red currant
Rotkohl red cabbage
Rotwein red wine
Rotwild (Tier) red deer
Rübe turnip
Rücken saddle

4268184

Rücksichtnahme considerateness
ruhig quiet, restful
Rühreier scrambled eggs
Rührglas mixing glass
Russe/Russin Russian
russisch Russian
Russland Russia

S

Safran saffron
Saft juice
saftig juicy
Sahne cream
Salat (kalt angemachte Speise) salad
Salat (Pflanze) lettuce
Salatsoße dressing
Salbei sage
salzig salty
Salzkartoffeln boiled potatoes
Salzwasserfisch sea fish
samtig velvety
Sardelle anchovy/three anchovies
Sardine sardine
sättigend nourishing, rich
säubern to clean
Sauce sauce
sauer sour
Sauerkraut sauerkraut
säuerlich tart
Sauna sauna
Säure acidity
sautieren to sautee, to fry
Schaf (Tier) sheep
Schaf(fleisch) mutton
Schafkäse ewe's cheese
Schale peel
Schalotte shallot
scharf hot, spicy
Schaum (Bier) froth
Schaumwein sparkling wine
Scheck check, (BE) cheque
Scheibe slice
Schellfisch haddock
schicken to send
Schikoree Belgian endive, chicory
Schimmel mold, (BE) mould
schimmelig moldy, (BE) mouldy
Schinken ham
Schlafzimmer bedroom, sleeping room
schlagen to whip, to beat
schlagen (mit dem Schneebesen) to whisk
Schlagsahne whipped cream
Schleie tench
Schloss palace
Schlüssel key
Schlüsselkarte key card
schmackhaft tasty
Schmalz dripping
Schmelztiegel melting pot
Schminktisch dressing table
schmoren to braise
Schnecke snail
Schneebesen whisk
Schneidearten ways of cutting
schneiden to cut
schneiden (hier: in Scheiben ~) to slice
Schnittlauch (bei Verwendung als Küchenkraut) chives
Schnittlauch (als Pflanze) chive
Schnitzel escalope
Schokolade chocolate
Scholle plaice
schön beautiful
Schreibtisch desk
Schriftverkehr correspondence
Schuppe (hier: Fischschuppe) scale
Schüssel bowl
schütteln to shake
schwach weak
Schwamm sponge
schwarze Johannisbeere black currant
Schwarzwurzel (black) salsify
Schwede/Schwedin Swede
Schweden Sweden
schwedisch Swedish
Schwein (Tier) pig
Schwein(efleisch) pork
schwenken (sautieren) to sautee, to fry
Scone (mürbeteigähnliches Gebäck) scone
Seetang seaweed
Seezunge sole
Sehenswürdigkeit sight
sehr very
Seife soap
Sekt sparkling wine
Sektflöte flute
Sektkühler champagne bucket
Sellerie (Knollen~) celeriac, German celery
Sellerie (Stangen~) celery
September September
Service service
servieren to serve
Serviette napkin
Shaker shaker
Shampoo shampoo
Sherry sherry
sich entschuldigen to apologize
Sieb sieve
Silberbesteck silverware
Silvester New Year's Eve
Sirup sirup, (BE) syrup
Sitz seat
Skandinavien Scandinavia
skandinavisch Scandinavian
Slowake/Slowakin Slovak
Slowakei Slovakia
slowakisch Slovak
Sofa couch, settee, sofa
Sofakissen cushion
sofort at once, immediately
Sojabohnen soybeans
Sorbet sherbet, sorbet
Soße sauce
Spanferkel suckling pig
Spanien Spain
Spanier/-in Spaniard
spanisch Spanish
Spargel asparagus
Spargelspitze asparagus tip
Speck bacon
Speisenkarte menu
sperren (Konto, Kreditkarte o. Ä.) to freeze
Spezialität specialty, (BE) speciality
Spiegel mirror
Spiegelei fried egg
Spiegelei (nur von einer Seite gebraten) fried egg sunny side up
Spinat spinach
Spirituose liquor, (BE) spirit
sprießen to sprout
Spritzer dash
Spritzflasche dash bottle
Spross shoot, sprout
Stadion stadium
Stadt town
Stadtrand (am Stadtrand) (MZ) outskirts (on the outskirts)
Stammgast regular (guest)
Stammwürze original gravity
Stapel stack (of plates)
stark strong
Steak steak
Steckdose socket
Steinbutt turbot
Steingarnele prawn
Steinpilz flat mushroom, mushroom
Steppdecke quilt
Stern star (Zweisternerestaurant: two-star restaurant)
Steuer tax
Stil (im Stile von ...) style (styled like ...)
stilvoll stylish
stopfen, füllen to stuff
Stöpsel plug
Stör sturgeon
Strainer strainer
Strandkrabbe crab
Straßenbahn streetcar, (BE) tram
Strauß ostrich
Stück (hier: Seife) cake
Suppe soup
süß sweet
Süße sweetness
Süßstoff sweetener
Süßwasserfisch freshwater fish

T

Tablett tray
Tag day
Tag der Arbeit May Bank Holiday
Tag der Deutschen Einheit Day of German Unity
Tannin tannin
tanninhaltig tannic
Tasse (groß) mug / (normal) cup

Taube pigeon
Taxistand taxi stand
Tee tea
Teekanne tea pot
Teelöffel tea spoon
Teigwaren pasta
Telefon telephone
Telefonbuch telephone directory
Telefonhörer receiver
Telefonverzeichnis telephone directory
Tennisplatz tennis court
Teppich (groß) carpet / (Brücke, Läufer) rug
Teppichboden carpet
teuer expensive
Theater theater, (BE) theatre
Theke bar, counter
Thermostat thermostat
Thunfisch tuna
Thymian thyme
Tiefgarage underground car park
Tier animal
Toastständer toast rack
Toilette bathroom
Toilette comfort room, CR
Toilette gentlemen's room/ladies' room
Toilette rest room
Toilette toilet
Toilettenpapier toilet roll, toilet paper
Toilettensitz toilet seat
Tomate(n) tomato(es)
traditionell traditional
Träger porter
tränken (mit) to soak (in)
Traube grape
Treber draff, sediment
Trieb shoot, sprout
Trinkbecher (große Tasse) mug
Trinkgeld tip
Trinkhalm straw
Tropfen drop
trüb (Bier/Wein) cloudy
Trüffel truffle
Truthahn turkey
Tscheche/Tschechin Czech
tschechisch Czech
Tschechische Republik Czech Republic

U

U-Bahn subway, (BE) underground, tube
überbacken to gratinate
übergar too done, too well done
überqueren to cross
Überweg (ebenerdig) level crossing
Umgebung (MZ) sourroundings
umgehend at once, immediately
umhüllen to coat, to encase
ummanteln to coat, to encase
umrühren to stir
Umsicht considerateness
umtauschen to change
unaufdringlich unobtrusive
Ungar/-in Hungarian
ungarisch Hungarian
Ungarn Hungary
Unterart variety
untergärig bottom-fermented beer / bottom fermenting yeast
Unterschrift signature
Untertasse saucer

V

Vanille vanilla
Vanillecreme custard
Vegetarier/-in vegetarian
vegetarisch vegetarian
Ventilator fan
Venusmuschel clam
Verabschiedung (in einem Brief) complimentary close
verbieten to prohibit
verblassen to fade
verdorben spoilt
versalzen oversalted
Versicherung(sgesellschaft) insurance company
Verwaltung administration
Verzehr consumption
verzehren to consume
viel a lot of ...
Viertel quarter (one/a quarter of ...)
Vietnam Vietnam
Vietnamese/Vietnamesin Vietnamese
vietnamesisch Vietnamese
Vollbier ordinary beer
vollmundig rich
Vorbereitungsarten ways of preparation
Vorhang curtain
vorherrschen to prevail
Vorliebe preference
Vorspeise appetizer

W

Wacholderbeere juniper berry
Wachtel quail
Waffel waffle
Wald wood
Waldmeister woodruff
Walnuss walnut
Waschbecken washbasin
Wäsche laundry
Wäscherei launderette
Waschlappen flannel
Wasserhahn faucet, (BE) tap
Wasserkasten (Toilette) cistern
Wassermelone water melon
wechseln to change
Wecker alarm clock
Weiberfastnacht Carnival Thursday
weich soft, fluffy
Weihnachten christmas
Wein (Getränk) wine / (Pflanze) vine
Weinbeere grape
Weinberg vinyard, winery, estate
Weingut vinyard, winery, estate
Weinkarte wine list
Weinkühler wine bucket
Weinstock vine
weiße Rübe turnip
Weißkohl white cabbage
Weißwein white wine
weit far (farther, farthest / further, furthest)
weitläufig extensive
Weizen wheat
Whiskyglas tumbler
wie bei Muttern traditional, classic
Wien Vienna
Wiesenchampignon field mushroom
Wild (Fleisch) venison / (Tier) deer
Wildbret game
Wildgeflügel feathered game
Wildschwein wild boar
Wirsing Savoy cabbage
Wohnzimmer living room
wolfen, durch den Wolf drehen to grind, (BE) to mince
Würfel cube
würfeln to cube
Würze (Bier) wort
würzen to season
würzig spicy

Z

zäh tough
Zahl number
Zahnbürste toothbrush
Zahnpasta toothpaste
Zahnstocher toothpick
Zapfhahn tap
zart tender, soft, fine
Zeit time
Zeit (hier: geschichtlicher Zeitabschnitt) period
Zentralheizung central heating
Zentrum center, (BE) centre
zerstoßenes Eis crushed ice
ziemlich quite
Zimt cinnamon
Zitrone lemon
zögerlich reluctant
Zucchini zucchini, (BE) courgette
Zuchtchampignon button mushroom
züchten to breed (bred/bred)
Zuckerdose sugar bowl
Zuckererbsen sugar peas
Zuckerersatzstoff sweetener
zuckerkrank diabetic
Zunge tongue
zurückhaltend reluctant
Zutaten ingredients
zweiter Weihnachtstag Boxing Day
Zwiebel onion

Vocabulary: English – German

(BE) Nur im britischen Englisch gebräuchlich.

(MZ) Dieses Wort wird nur in der Mehrzahl gebraucht.

A

a lot of ... viel
to accept akzeptieren, annehmen
acidity Säure
to add hinzufügen
administration Verwaltung
after nach
air conditioned mit Klimaanlage
air conditioning Klimaanlage
airport Flughafen
alarm clock Wecker
alcohol Alkohol
alcohol contents (high/low ~) Alkoholgehalt (hoher/niedriger ~)
alcohol free alkoholfrei
alcoholic alkoholhaltig, alkoholisch
All Saints' Day Allerheiligen
alley Gasse
almond Mandel
along entlang
America Amerika
American Amerikaner/-in, amerikanisch
anchovy/three anchovies Sardelle(n)
anglican anglikanisch
animal Tier
anise Anis (Pflanze)
aniseed Anis(samen)
application Bewerbung
to apply for sich bewerben um
to apologize sich entschuldigen
appetizer Appetitanreger, Vorspeise
apple Apfel
apricot Aprikose
April April
area Gebiet
arrival Ankunft
artichoke Artischocke
Ascension Day Christi Himmelfahrt
ashtray Aschenbecher
Asia Asien
Asian Asiate/Asiatin, asiatisch
to ask beauftragen, bitten
asparagus Spargel
asparagus tips Spargelspitzen
to assimilate angleichen, assimilieren
astonishing erstaunlich
at once sofort, umgehend
attack Angriff
attentive aufmerksam
aubergine Aubergine
au gratin gratiniert
August August
avenue Allee

B

bacon Speck
baggage Gepäck
to bake backen
baked (jacket) potato Folienkartoffel
balance Ausgewogenheit, Balance
balanced abgestimmt, ausgewogen
banana Banane
bank Bank (Geldinstitut)
bank transfer Banküberweisung
bar Bar, Theke
bar spoon Barlöffel
to barbecue grillen (nur Fleisch)
barley Gerste
basic grundsätzlich
basil Basilikum
bathroom Badezimmer
bathroom Toilette
bay leaf/leaves Lorbeerblatt/-blätter
bean Bohne
to beat schlagen
beautiful schön
bed Bett
bed room Schlafzimmer
bed table Nachttisch
beef Ochsenfleisch, Rind(fleisch)
beer Bier
beer warmer Bierwärmer
beetroot Rote Bete
behind hinter
Belgian endive Chicorée
bench Bank (Sitzmöbel)
berry/-ies Beere(n)
bewerben (sich bewerben um) to apply for
Bewerbung application
big groß
bill (vorwiegend BE) Rechnung / Banknote, Geldschein
bitter bitter
black currant schwarze Johannisbeere
black pudding Blutwurst
black salsify Schwarzwurzeln
blackberry/-ies Brombeere(n)
blender Mixer
blood Blut
blouse Bluse
blueberry/-ies Blaubeere(n), Heidelbeere(n)
body Körper
body of the letter Brieftext
Bohemia Böhmen
Bohemian Böhme/Böhmin, böhmisch
to boil kochen (bei 100 °C in Wasser garen)
boiled egg gekochtes Ei
boiled jacket potatoes Pellkartoffeln
boiled potatoes Salzkartoffeln
to book bestellen, buchen, reservieren
booking Bestellung, Buchung, Reservierung
bottle opener Flaschenöffner
bottom fermenting (yeast) untergärig(e Hefe)
bottom-fermented (beer) untergärig(es Bier)
bouillon klare Brühe
bowl Schüssel
Boxing Day zweiter Weihnachtstag
brain Hirn
to braise schmoren
bread Brot
bread basket Brotkorb
breaded paniert
breakfast cup Frühstückstasse
breast Brust
to breed (bred/bred) züchten
brewery Brauerei
bright glänzend
Briton Brite/Britin
broad bean dicke Bohne
broccoli Brokkoli
to broil (AE) grillen
broth Bouillon, klare Brühe
Brussels sprouts Rosenkohl
buffet Büfett
building Gebäude
Burgundy Burgunder(wein)
burnt angebrannt
bus ride Busfahrt
business Geschäft
businessfriend Geschäftsfreund
busy geschäftig
butter dish Butterschälchen
butter knife Buttermesser
button mushroom Zuchtchampignon

C

cabbage Kohl
cake Kuchen/Stück (Seife)
calf Kalb (Tier)
calory/-ies Kalorie(n)
car park (BE) Parkplatz
carafe Karaffe
caramel Karamell
caraway Kümmel (Pflanze)
carawayseed Kümmel(samen)
carnation Nelke (Blume)
Carnival Monday Rosenmontag
Carnival Thursday Weiberfastnacht
carp Karpfen
carpet Teppich (groß), Teppichboden
carrot Möhre
cash bar
cash register Kasse
caste Kaste (religiöse und soziale Schicht)
castle Burg

cathedral Dom
catholic katholisch
cauliflower Blumenkohl
caviar Kaviar
Cayenne Cayennepfeffer
Cayenne pepper Cayennepfeffer
celeriac Knollensellerie
celery Stangensellerie
cemetery Friedhof
center Innenstadt, Zentrum
Central Europe Mitteleuropa
central heating Zentralheizung
central station Hauptbahnhof
centre (BE) Innenstadt, Zentrum
cereal Getreideprodukte
champagne Champagner
champagne bucket Sektkühler
champignon Champignon
to change auswechseln, umtauschen, wechseln
chanterelle Pfifferling
chard Mangold
to charge berechnen
check Rechnung, Scheck
cheese Käse
chef Koch (professionell)
cheque (BE) Scheck
cherry/-ies Kirsche(n)
chervil Kerbel
chestnut Esskastanie, Marone
chicken Huhn, Poularde
chicory Chicorée
chile Chili
chilli (BE) Chili
China China
Chinese cabbage Chinakohl
Chinese Chinese/Chinesin, chinesisch
chips (BE) Pommes frites
chive Schnittlauch (Pflanze)
chives Schnittlauch (bei Verwendung als Küchenkraut)
chocolate Schokolade
chocolate spread Nussnugataufstrich
choice Auswahl
to chop hacken
Christmas Day erster Weihnachtstag
Christmas Eve Heiligabend
church Kirche
chutney Chutney (ein würziges Mus aus klein geschnittenen Früchten und/ oder Gemüsen mit Essig, Gewürzen und Kräutern)
cinema Kino
cinnamon Zimt
cistern (Toilette) Wasserkasten
city Großstadt
clam Venusmuschel
claret Bordeaux(wein) (rot)
classic wie bei Muttern
to clean säubern
cleaners (MZ) Reinigung
clear klar
cloakroom Garderobe
close (to) nahe (bei)
clotted cream eingedickte Sahne
cloudy trüb
clove Nelke (Gewürz)
coaster Bierdeckel
coat hanger Kleiderbügel
coat stand Kleiderständer
to coat umhüllen, ummanteln
coated with bread crumbs paniert
cocktail glass Cocktailglas
cocktail stick Cocktailstick
coconut Kokosnuss
cod Kabeljau
coffee Kaffee
coffee pot Kaffeekanne
coffee table Beistelltisch
cold cuts Aufschnitt
cold kalt
coloring Farbe, Farbstoff
colouring (BE) Farbe, Farbstoff
comb Kamm
combination Kombination
comfort room Toilette
to complain sich beschweren
complimentary close Verabschiedung (in einem Brief)
condiments Menage (als Zutat)
to confirm bestätigen
confirmation Bestätigung
considerateness Rücksichtnahme, Umsicht
consommé Consommé, Kraftbrühe
to consume konsumieren, verzehren
consumption Verzehr
to cook garen, kochen
cook Koch (allgemein)
cooked gegart, gekocht
cooking Essen, Kochen, Küche (Art der Speisenzubereitung)
copper Kupfer
cork Korken
corkscrew Korkenzieher
corn Getreide, Mais
to corn pökeln
corner Ecke
corner seat Eckbank
cornflakes Cornflakes
correspondence Briefverkehr, Schriftverkehr
cosy (BE) behaglich, bequem
couch Couch, Sofa
counter Theke
to counterbalance ausgleichen
country Land
courgette (BE) Zucchini
course Gang
courteous höflich
cover charge Gedeck(preis)
cover Couvert
cow Rind (Tier)
cozy behaglich, bequem
CR (comfort room) Toilette
crab Strandkrabbe
crawfish Languste
crayfish Krebs
cream Creme/Krem, Sahne
credit card Kreditkarte
crispy knackig
crockery Geschirr
croissant Croissant
croquette potatoes Kartoffelkroketten
to cross überqueren
to crown krönen
cruet (stand) Menage (als Gegenstand)
crunchy knusprig
crushed ice Crasheis, gestoßenes Eis
cube Würfel
to cube würfeln, in Würfel schneiden
cucumber Gurke
cuisine Essen, Küche (Art der Speisenzubereitung)
culinary kulinarisch
culture Kultur
cup Tasse (normal)
curd Quark
curly kale Grünkohl
Curriculum Vitae Lebenslauf
curry Curry (Gewürzmischung)
curtain Gardine, Vorhang
cushion Sofakissen
custard englische Creme, Vanillecreme
to cut schneiden
cutlery Besteck
cutlery chest Besteckschrank
cutlet Kotelett
CV (Curriculum Vitae) Lebenslauf
Czech Republic Tschechische Republik
Czech Tscheche/Tschechin, tschechisch

D

Dane Däne/Dänin
Danish dänischdark dunkel
dash Spritzer
dash bottle Spritzflasche
date Datum
day Tag
Day of German Unity Tag der Deutschen Einheit
Day of Repentance Buß- und Bettag
decaffeinated entkoffeiniert
to decant dekantieren
decanter Karaffe
December Dezember
to decorate dekorieren
decoration Dekoration
decorative dekorativ
to deep-fry frittieren
deer Wild (Tier)
Denmark Dänemark
departure Abfahrt, Abflug
desk Schreibtisch
dessert Dessert, Nachspeise
diabetes Diabetes
diabetic Diabetiker, zuckerkrank
to dice würfeln, in Würfel schneiden
diet Diät, Ernährung

dietary rules Ernährungsvorschriften
dill Dill
dish Gericht
to dominate dominieren
doorman Pförtner
double bed Doppelbett
draff Treber
drape Gardine
to dress (besonders BE) anmachen (z. B. Salat)
dressing Salatsoße
dressing table Schminktisch
dripping Schmalz
drop Tropfen
dry herb
dry-cleaning chemische Reinigung
duck Ente
dull fad
dumpling Kloß, Knödel
Dutch holländisch

E

to ease someone's mind erleichtern
East-Asia Ostasien
Easter Ostern
eel Aal
egg Ei
egg-cup Eierbecher
egg plant (BE) Aubergine
egg white Eiklar
Eire Irland (gälischer Name Irlands)
electric elektrisch
elegant elegant
elevator Aufzug
elk europäischer Elch
embarrassing peinlich
to empty ausleeren
Enc. Anlage (zu einem Brief)
to encase einhüllen, ummanteln, umhüllen
enclosure Anlage (zu einem Brief)
Encs. Anlagen (zu einem Brief)
endive Endivie
enquiry Anfrage
equipment Ausstattung, Einrichtung (technisch)
equipped with ausgestattet mit
escalope Schnitzel
estate Weinberg, Weingut (Ort, wo angepflanzt und produziert wird)
Europe Europa
European Europäer/-in, europäisch
ewe's cheese Schafkäse
exhibition Ausstellung
expensive teuer
explicit (Adjektiv) ausdrücklich
explicitly (Adverb) ausdrücklich
exposition ground Ausstellungsgelände, Messegelände
exposition Messe (Ausstellung)
extensive ausgedehnt, weitläufig

F

facility/-ies Einrichtung(en), Hoteleinrichtung(en), Möglichkeit(en)
factory Fabrik
to fade verblassen
fair ground Ausstellungsgelände, Messegelände
fair Messe (Ausstellung)
fallow deer Damwild (Tier)
fan Ventilator
far (farther, farthest/further, furthest) weit
fashion Mode
to fast fasten
fat Fett
fat-free mager
faucet Wasserhahn
fault Fehler
Feast of Corpus Christi Fronleichnam
feathered game Wildgeflügel
February Februar
fennel Fenchel
to ferment fermentieren, gären
fermentation Gärung
field mushroom Wiesenchampignon
fig Feige
Filipino Philippine/Philippinin, philippinisch
to fill einfüllen, füllen
fillet Filet
to fillet filetieren, filieren
to filter filtern
fin Flosse
fine fein, gut, zart
finger biscuit Löffelbiskuit
finish Abgang
Finland Finnland
Finnish finnisch
fireplace Kamin
fish/three fish (Anzahl), **three fishes** (Arten) Fisch
fish broth Court-bouillon
fish course Fischgang
to flambé flambieren
flambé flambiert
flambéed flambiert
flannel Waschlappen
flat flach
flat mushroom Steinpilz
to flavor aromatisieren
to flavour (BE) aromatisieren
florist's Blumenhandlung
flour Mehl
flowery blumig
fluffy weich
flute Sektflöte
food Ernährung, Essen, Küche (Art der Speisenzubereitung)
food Essen, Lebensmittel
fortified wine aufgespriteter Wein
France Frankreich
frankly ehrlich, offen gesagt
to freeze sperren (Konto, Kreditkarte o. Ä.)
French bean grüne Bohne
French französisch
French fries Pommes frites
fresh frisch
freshwater fish Süßwasserfisch
fried egg Spiegelei
fried egg sunny side up Spiegelei (nur von einer Seite gebraten)
fried potatoes Bratkartoffeln
friendly freundlich
froth Schaum (Bier)
fruit Obst
fruit knife Früchtemesser
fruit preserve Konfitüre, Marmelade
fruit press Fruchtpresse
fruity fruchtig
to fry braten (kurz)
fullbodied körperreich
fully booked ausgebucht
furnished möbliert
furnishing Möblierung

G

game Wildbret
garbage bin Abfalleimer
garlic Knoblauch
to garnish garnieren
general impression Gesamtbild
gentlemen's room Toilette (Herren)
German celery Knollensellerie
to germinate keimen
gherkin (BE) Gewürzgurke
ginger Ingwer
glass Glas
glassware Gläser
to glaze glasieren
golf course Golfplatz
good and solid deftig
good for you gesund (zur Beschreibung von Lebensmitteln)
Good Friday Karfreitag
goose/geese Gans/Gänse
grain Getreide
granola Müsli
grape Traube, Weinbeere
grapefruit Grapefruit, Pampelmuse
to gratinate gratinieren, überbacken
gratinated gratiniert
Great Britain Großbritannien
great großartig
Greece Griechenland
Greek Grieche/Griechin, griechisch
green kale Grünkohl
greenish (blueish, -ish) grünlich (bläulich, -lich)
to grill (BE) grillen
grind wolfen, durch den Wolf drehen
guinea fowl Perlhuhn

H

haddock Schellfisch
half (one/a half of ...) Hälfte
half timbered (house) Fachwerk(haus)

halibut Heilbutt
ham Schinken
Hamilton Mixer
hard hart
hare Hase
hash browns (AE) Bratkartoffeln (aus Streifen von rohen Kartoffeln)
hawk Falke
hazelnut Haselnuss
head Krone (Bier)
headache Kopfschmerzen
health Gesundheit
heart Herz
hearty herzhaft
heating Heizung
herb Kraut
herring Hering
hock Rheinwein
honeydew melon Honigmelone
hop Hopfen (Pflanze)
hoppy (salopp) hopfenbetont
hops Hopfen (getrocknet, als Brauzutat)
horseradish Meerrettich
hot heiß, scharf
hot chocolate (Trink-)Schokolade
hotel and catering business Hotel- und Gaststättengewerbe
house Haus (als Gebäude nur für Ein-/Zweifamilienhäuser bzw. Reihenhäuser)
huckleberry/-ies amerikanische Heidelbeere(n)
Hungarian Ungar/-in, ungarisch
Hungary Ungarn

I

Iberian Peninsula Iberische Halbinsel
ice cream Eis(creme)
ice cube Eiswürfel
icecube box Eisbox
ice-tongs Eiszange
immediately sofort, umgehend
to include einschließen
India Indien
Indian Inder/-in, Indianer/-in
Indian indisch/indianisch
Indonesia Indonesien
Indonesian Indonesier/-in, indonesisch
ingredients Zutaten
inhibition Hemmung
inquiry Anfrage
insurance company Versicherung (sgesellschaft)
interior Inneneinrichtung
international international
Ireland Irland
Islam Islam
Islamic islamisch
island Insel
Italian Italiener/-in, italienisch
Italy Italien
item Punkt, Posten (auf einer Rechnung)

J

jacket potatoes Pellkartoffeln
jam Konfitüre, Marmelade
January Januar
Japan Japan
Japanese Japaner/-in, japanisch
jasmin Jasmin
jelly Gelee
Jew Jude/Jüdin
Jewish jüdisch
jigger Messbecher
Judaism Judentum
juice Saft
juicy saftig
July Juli
June Juni
juniper berry/-ies Wacholderbeere(n)

K

kale Grünkohl
key Schlüssel
key card Schlüsselkarte
kidney Niere
to kiln-dry darren
kitchen Küche (Ort)
knuckle Hachse, Haxe
kohlrabi Kohlrabi

L

label Etikett
to lace aromatisieren (mit Spirituosen)
ladies' room Toilette (Damen)
lamb Lamm, Lammfleisch
lamb's lettuce Feldsalat
lamp Lampe
Latin America Lateinamerika
launderette Wäscherei
laundry Wäsche
lean mager
to leave abreisen
leek Lauch, Porree
left links
leg Keule
legal legal, rechtens
lemon Zitrone
Lent Fastenzeit
lentil Linse (Hülsenfrucht)
lettuce Salat (Pflanze)
level crossing Überweg (ebenerdig)
level Niveau
lift (BE) Aufzug
light hell (Wein)
light leicht
lights (kulinarisch) (MZ) Lunge
lime Limone
liqueur Likör
liquid Flüssigkeit
liquor Spirituose
listed building denkmalgeschütztes Gebäude
liter Liter
litre (BE) Liter
liver Leber
living room Wohnzimmer
lobster Hummer
local lokal, örtlich
local public transportation system ÖPNV (öffentlicher Personennahverkehr)
local public transport system (BE) ÖPNV (öffentlicher Personennahverkehr)
to be located liegen (hier: örtliche Platzierung)
location Lage
low in fat mager
low-fat mager, mit niedrigem Fettgehalt
low-in-calories kalorienarm
lukewarm lauwarm
lunch Mittagessen
luncheon Mittagessen (sprachlich korrekte, wenn auch kaum noch gebräuchliche Form)
lung(s) Lunge (Organ)

M

mackerel Makrele
main hauptsächlich
main course Hauptgang
maize (BE) Mais
major hauptsächlich
to make a nuisance of (oneself/ herself ...) lästig fallen
malt Malz
malty malzig
manager Geschäftsführer
maple sirup Ahornsirup
March März
to marinade marinieren
to marinate marinieren
marjoram Majoran
marmalade Orangenmarmelade (bitter, mit Schalenstücken)
marrow Mark
marvellous großartig
mash Maische
to mash maischen, pürieren
mashed potatoes Kartoffelbrei, Kartoffelpüree
mass Messe (relig.)
matched abgestimmt
mattress Matratze
maturation Reifung
mature reif
May Mai
May Bank Holiday Erster Mai (Tag der Arbeit)
meal Essen, Mahl, Mahlzeit
meal Gericht
measure Maß, Maßeinheit
meat Fleisch
medallion Medaillon
Mediterranean Countries Mittelmeerländer
Mediterranean Sea Mittelmeer
medium medium (Steak)
melon Melone
melting pot Schmelztiegel

4268190

menu Speisenkarte
Mexican Mexikaner/-in, mexikanisch
Mexico Mexiko
mild mild
milk Milch
milk jug Milchkännchen
mince (BE) wolfen, durch den Wolf drehen
minibar Minibar
mint Minze
mirror Spiegel
Miss (in einer Anrede, z. B. Brief) Fräulein
to miss fehlen
to mix mischen, mixen
mixer Mixer
mixing glass Rührglas, Mixglas
mocha Mokka
modern modern
mold Form/Schimmel
moldy schimmelig
month Monat
moose amerikanischer Elch
morel Morchel
Moselle Mosel (Fluss u. Wein)
mould (BE) Form
mould (BE) Schimmel
mouldy (BE) schimmelig
movement Bewegung
Mr (in einer Anrede, z. B. Brief) Herr
Mrs (in einer Anrede, z. B. Brief) Frau
mug Becher, große Tasse, Trinkbecher
mugwort Beifuß
multi storey car park Parkhaus
multigym Fitnessraum
museum Museum
mushroom Pilz, Champignon, Steinpilz
mussel Miesmuschel
must Most
mutton Hammel(fleisch), Schaf(fleisch)

N

napkin Serviette
near nah
neighborhood Nachbarschaft
neighbourhood (BE) Nachbarschaft
New Year's Day Neujahr
New Year's Eve Silvester
next to neben
no-smoking area Menage
non-alcoholic alkoholfrei
Norway Norwegen
Norwegian Norweger/-in, norwegisch
nose Nase (= Geruch)
not done nicht gar
note (BE) Banknote, Geldschein
nourishing sättigend
November November
number Anzahl, Zahl
nutmeg Muskatnuss

O

oatmeal Haferflocken
oats Hafer
October Oktober
octupus Krake
offal Innereien
offer Angebot
to offer anbieten
office Büro
oil Öl
old alt
old fashioned altmodisch
olive Olive
omelett Omelett
on the corner an der Ecke
on the outskirts am Stadtrand
on the side nebenbei, nebenher
onion Zwiebel
open sandwich Butterbrot (offen)
opening hours Öffnungszeiten
opera Oper
orange Apfelsine
orange juice Orangensaft
order Bestellung, Reihenfolge
to order bestellen
ordinary beer Vollbier
oregano Oregano
original gravity Stammwürze
outskirts (MZ) Stadtrand
to overlook Aussicht haben/bieten, Blick haben/bieten
oversalted versalzen
owl Eule
ox Ochse (Tier)

P

Pacific Ocean Pazifischer Ozean
palace Schloss
palate Gaumen
pale hell (Bier)
pancake Pfannkuchen
park Park
park grounds Parkanlagen
parking lot Parkplatz
parsley Petersilie
parsnip Paprika
partridge Rebhuhn
to pass through (a sieve, a strainer ...) hindurchgeben (durch Sieb, Strainer ...)
pasta Nudeln, Teigwaren
paste Paste
pea Erbse
peaceful friedlich
peach/-es Pfirsich
peanut Erdnuss
pear Birne
pedestrians' area Fußgängerzone
pedestrians' crossing Fußgängerüberweg
peel Schale
peninsula Halbinsel
pepper Paprika, Pfeffer
percent, per cent Prozent
period Periode, Zeit (geschichtlicher Zeitabschnitt)
pheasant Fasan
Philippine Philippine/Philippinin, philippinisch
Philippines Philippinen
pickle (AE) Gewürzgurke
to pickle einlegen
pie Pastete
pieces of meat Fleischteile
pig Schwein (Tier)
pigeon Taube
pike Hecht
pillow Kopfkissen
pimento Nelkenpfeffer, Piment
pineapple Ananas
pistachio Pistazie
plaice Scholle
plane Flugzeug
plant Fabrik
plates and dishes Geschirr
plug Stöpsel
plum Pflaume
to poach pochieren
poached egg pochiertes Ei
Poland Polen
Pole Pole/Polin
Polish polnisch
politc höflich
to pop up (salopp) hochflitzen
poppy Mohn (Pflanze)
poppy seed Mohn(samen)
popular beliebt, populär
pork Schwein(efleisch)
porridge Haferbrei
port Portwein
porter Gepäckträger
Portugal Portugal
Portuguese Portugiese/Portugiesin, portugiesisch
potato(es) Kartoffel(n)
potato croquettes Kartoffelkroketten
poultry Geflügel
to pour gießen
prawn Steingarnele
preference Vorliebe
presentation Darbietung, Präsentation
preservative Konservierungsmittel
preserve dish Marmeladentöpfchen
preserve Konserve (hier: Marmelade, Gelee usw.)
to preserve konservieren
to prevail vorherrschen
price Preis (Geld)
prize Preis (Gewinn)
to prohibit verbieten
protestant evangelisch, protestantisch
prune Backpflaume
public transport Nahverkehr
pudding Pudding (= in der Form gegarte Speise; auch im Englischen inzwischen als Synonym für *Flammeri* gebraucht)

puff pastry Blätterteig
pumpkin Kürbis

Q

quail Wachtel
quarter (one/a quarter of ...) Viertel
quiet ruhig
quilt Steppdecke
quince Quitte
quite ziemlich

R

rabbit Kaninchen
radiator Heizkörper
radish/-es Radieschen
ragout Ragout
raisin Rosine
rare englisch (Steak)
raspberry/-ies Himbeere(n)
raw blau, blutig (Steak)
raw roh
razor Rasierer
razorblade Rasierklinge
reading lamp Leselampe
receipt Kassenbon, Kassenbeleg
receiver Telefonhörer
receptionist Empfangsdame, -herr
recipe Rezept
to recommend empfehlen
recommendation Empfehlung
red cabbage Rotkohl
red currant rote Johannisbeere
red deer Rotwild (Tier)
red wine Rotwein
reference initials Bezugszeichen
refreshing erfrischend
refusal Absage, Ablehnung
regional regional
regular regelmäßig
regular (guest) Stammgast
reluctant zögerlich, zurückhaltend
reminder Mahnung
to replace auswechseln, ersetzen
reservation Bestellung, Buchung, Reservierung
to reserve reservieren
rest room Toilette
restaurant Restaurant
restful friedlich, ruhig
Rhine wine Rheinwein
rhubarb Rhabarber
rice Reis
rich kalorienreich, sättigend, vollmundig
right rechts
ripe reif
to roast braten (lang)
roe Rogen
roe deer Rehwild (Tier)
rosé Rosé
rosemary Rosmarin
rough rau
rug Läufer (Teppich)
Russia Russland
Russian Russe/Russin, russisch
rye Roggen

S

saddle Rücken
saffron Safran
sage Salbei
salad Salat (kalt angemachte Speise)
salmon Lachs
salsify Schwarzwurzel
salty salzig
salutation Anrede (in einem Brief)
sandwich Butterbrot (zugeklappt)
sardine Sardine
sauce Soße
saucer Untertasse
sauerkraut Sauerkraut
sauna Sauna
sausage Bratwurst
sausage slices Aufschnitt
savory Bohnenkraut
Savoy cabbage Wirsing
scale Fischschuppe
scallop Jakobsmuschel
Scandinavia Skandinavien
Scandinavian skandinavisch
scone Scone (mürbteigähnliches Gebäck)
scrambled eggs Rühreier
sea fish Salzwasserfisch
to season würzen
seat Platz (z. B. im Restaurant), Sitz
seaweed Seetang
sediment Bodensatz, Treber
selection Auswahl
to send schicken
sender's name Absender
sensation Empfindung
September September
sequence Reihenfolge
to serve servieren
service Bedienung, Dienstleistung, Service
service Gottesdienst
service charge Bedienungsgeld
serving hatch Durchreiche
settee Couch, Sofa
to shake schütteln
shaker Mixbecher, Shaker
shallot Schalotte
shampoo Shampoo
sheep Schaf (Tier)
sheet Bettlaken
shelf Regal
shellfish Krusten- und Schaltiere
sherbet Sorbet
sherry Sherry
shirt Hemd
shoot Spross, Trieb
shopping area Einkaufszone
shopping gallery Einkaufspassage
shopping mall Einkaufspassage
shower Dusche, Handdusche
shrimp Garnele
side dish Beilage
side knife Brotmesser (zum Streichen)
side order Beilage
side plate Brotteller
sieve Sieb
to sieve durchsieben
sight Sehenswürdigkeit
signature Unterschrift
silverware Besteck (Silber)
single bed Einzelbett
sirup / (BE) syrup Sirup
to be situated liegen (hier: örtliche Platzierung)
skim milk fettarme Milch
skirt Rock
sleeping room Schlafzimmer
slice Scheibe
to slice in Scheiben schneiden
Slovak Slowake/Slowakin, slowakisch
Slovakia Slowakei
to smoke räuchern
snail Schnecke
to soak tränken
soap Seife
socket Steckdose
sofa Couch, Sofa
soft weich, zart
sole Seezunge
solid hart
sorbet Sorbet
soup Suppe
sour sauer
soybean Sojabohne
Spain Spanien
Spaniard Spanier/-in
Spanish spanisch
sparkling wine Schaumwein, Sekt
speciality (BE) Spezialität
specialty Spezialität
spice Gewürz
spicy gewürzt, pikant, scharf, würzig
spinach Spinat
spirit (BE) Spirituose
spoilt verdorben
sponge Schwamm
spoon Löffel
to sprinkle beträufeln
sprout Spross, Trieb
to sprout sprießen
to squeeze ausdrücken
stack (of plates) Stapel
stadium Stadion
stale abgestanden
staple diet Hauptnahrung(smittel)
star (two-star restaurant) Stern (Zweisternerestaurant)
station Bahnhof
steak Steak
to steam dämpfen
stew Ragout
to stew dünsten

4268192